MACHINE LEARNING OF INDUCTIVE BIAS

THE KLUWER INTERNATIONAL SERIES
IN ENGINEERING AND COMPUTER SCIENCE

KNOWLEDGE REPRESENTATION, LEARNING AND EXPERT SYSTEMS

Consulting Editor

Tom M. Mitchell

MACHINE LEARNING
OF
INDUCTIVE BIAS

by

Paul E. Utgoff
University of Massachusetts
Amherst, Massachusetts

KLUWER ACADEMIC PUBLISHERS
Boston / Dordrecht / Lancaster

Distributors for North America:
Kluwer Academic Publishers
101 Philip Drive
Assinippi Park
Norwell, Massachusetts 02061, USA

Distributors for the UK and Ireland:
Kluwer Academic Publishers
MTP Press Limited
Falcon House, Queen Square
Lancaster LA1 1RN, UNITED KINGDOM

Distributors for all other countries:
Kluwer Academic Publishers Group
Distribution Centre
Post Office Box 322
3300 AH Dordrecht, THE NETHERLANDS

Library of Congress Cataloging-in-Publication Data

Utgoff, Paul E., 1951-
  Machine learning of inductive bias.

  (The Kluwer international series in engineering and
computer science. Knowledge representation, learning
and expert systems)
  Includes index.
  1. Machine learning. 2. Artificial intelligence—
Data processing. I. Title. II. Title: Inductive bias.
III. Series.
Q325.U74 1986   006.3'1   86–10653
ISBN 0–89838–223–8

CONTENTS

List of Figures

List of Tables

Preface

This book is based on the author's Ph.D. dissertation[56]. The thesis research was conducted while the author was a graduate student in the Department of Computer Science at Rutgers University. The book was prepared at the University of Massachusetts at Amherst where the author is currently an Assistant Professor in the Department of Computer and Information Science.

Programs that learn concepts from examples are guided not only by the examples (and counterexamples) that they observe, but also by <u>bias</u> that determines which concept is to be considered as following best from the observations. Selection of a concept represents an inductive leap because the concept then indicates the classification of instances that have not yet been observed by the learning program. Learning programs that make undesirable inductive leaps do so due to undesirable bias. The research problem addressed here is to show how a learning program can learn a desirable inductive bias.

The thesis is that search for appropriate bias is itself a major part of the learning task, and that mechanical procedures can be constructed that conduct a well-directed search for an appropriate bias. This is believable because users of learning programs are observed to search for an appropriate bias. The user (usually the program author) generates a bias and tests the learning program. If the learning program makes acceptable inductive leaps then the program is deemed successful. Otherwise, the user repeats the generate-and-test cycle. With each cycle however, the user possesses more knowledge about how well each bias has performed.

The RTA Method (Recommend, Translate, Assimilate) is developed to automate the search for a good bias. The method is based on the ability to identify and provide new needed descriptive ability. A program STABB is presented that uses the RTA Method in two different procedures. STABB augments the LEX learning program by giving LEX the ability to learn its own inductive bias.

The main result is the demonstration that the search for a good bias can indeed be performed mechanically. Secondary results are the RTA Method and the two procedures of STABB.

Acknowledgements

This work was supported by National Science Foundation Grant GMCS80-08889, National Institute of Health Grant RR-64309, Rutgers University Laboratory for Computer Science Research, and Siemens Research and Technology Laboratories.

I thank all the people who helped in so many ways:

The discussions with Tom Mitchell were illuminating and inspiring. The work on building LEX was an invaluable apprenticeship in both doing and reporting research. Tom's judgement in recognizing which ideas are worth pursuing is truly remarkable. I was inspired by Ran Banerji's constantly fresh and eager outlook on the field of Machine Learning. His technical excellence, humor, and wisdom have provided valuable guidance. Saul Amarel's ability to isolate important research issues was very helpful. His skill in channeling research effort into sensibly-sized projects has saved me more than once. Sridharan's exacting standards, healthy skepticism, and interest in understanding played an important role in helping me understand my task more clearly. His ability to carefully separate what one means from what one says has helped many times to expose flaws. Bob Smith gave technical guidance and provided encouragement during the early stages of the research.

Rich Keller, Donna Nagel, Pat Schooley and I met regularly over several years to trade presentation of ideas. The in-depth discussions, careful readings, untempered criticism, and friendly commiseration have provided a unique source of criticism and encouragement.

The technical discussions with Tom Dietterich have been helpful. In addition, he has carefully read and commented on drafts of the dissertation and other related papers. Jaime Carbonell gave a careful reading and comprehensive comments on a draft of a related paper. The presentation here is greatly improved as a result. Smadar Kedar-Cabelli contributed a set of comments based on a reading of a draft. Tony Bonner pointed out technical problems with op50. Accompanying that were helpful discussions with Bruce Ladendorf and Michael Sims regarding the laws of exponents in the complex plane.

Sharad Saxena read the draft for this book and provided several incisive observations. The book is improved as a result.

Chuck Hedrick's ELISP (a LISP that uses the extended addressing capability of the DEC-20) was a pleasure to use. He provided prompt repair of ELISP bugs that surfaced during the programming phase of the research. JoAnn Gabinelli was always helpful in arranging meetings and helping to satisfy administrative details. The Rutgers Laboratory for Computer Science Research enhanced the working conditions by lending me a video terminal and modem for the last two years of the project.

Finally, my wife Karen and my two daughters Naomi and Emily have been a constant source of cheer, and support. They have made sacrifices both in undergoing the well known ups and downs of a Ph.D. aspirant and in foregoing a large amount of time together. They have helped me keep my head on straight; there is nothing like arriving home to a cheerful family to remind one of the secondary importance of academic pursuits.

MACHINE LEARNING OF INDUCTIVE BIAS

Chapter 1

Introduction

Work in Artificial Intelligence over the last 25 years has been devoted to the development and exploration of mechanisms that mimic behavior that is presumed to require intelligence. This work includes problem solving, game playing, theorem proving, reasoning, speech understanding, vision, natural language processing, and knowledge-based expert systems. One important dimension of this work is that some of the programs that mimic intelligence are capable of improving at a performance task, and some are not.

1.1 Machine Learning

A person or program that improves its performance is said to *learn*. Three intriguing aspects of learning are:

1. The ability to improve is a fascinating phenomenon. What mechanisms permit an entity to benefit from experience?

2. A program that can learn may be able to acquire knowledge that was not known to the program's author.

3. The ability of a program to learn lifts a large burden from authors of intelligent systems; the author is no longer required to produce and encode all the knowledge that a program is to have.

The ability both to acquire knowledge and to apply that knowledge in a way that can benefit performance is at the heart of intelligent behavior. There have been many successful learning programs to date. Samuel's

1

checkers player [47,48] improved its checker playing skill by learning to estimate the future value of a board position based on computable feature values. Koffman's program [18] learned to play positional games such as 4x4x4 ticktacktoe by learning the concept of a forced sequence of moves that result in a win. Waterman constructed a rule-based program [62] that became skilled at betting decisions in the game of draw poker. Winston's program [63] could learn concepts in the domain of structural descriptions, e.g. an arch. Michalski's A^q learning algorithm, embodied in the INDUCE program [25], has been applied to several concept learning tasks. In one celebrated experiment, his program learned classification rules for diagnosing soybean diseases. The induced rules were more succinct and did a better job of correctly classifying soybean diseases than rules that were formulated by human soybean pathology experts. The Meta-DENDRAL program [5,31] learned rules that predict cleavage points for chemical molecules subjected to electron bombardment in a mass spectrometer. Meta-DENDRAL "discovered new rules for three closely related families of structures for which rules had not been previously reported."[1] Lenat's EURISKO [21] learns concepts by discovery. Domains for EURISKO have included mathematics, LISP, naval fleet design (for a game), 3-dimensional VLSI design, and heuristics. Carbonell's program [6] learns word meanings from story and sentence context. Langley's BACON program [19] infers laws that are consistent with tables of data, e.g. Ohm's law. Mitchell's program LEX [36] improves its problem solving performance in the domain of integral calculus by learning the set of problem states to which each operator should be applied. Politakis constructed a program SEEK [43] that suggests improved rules for medical diagnosis by seeking inconsistencies in a rule base and proposing repairs to the rules. Sammut's MARVIN [46] learns concepts both from examples and by asking questions of the trainer.

The success of these and other learning programs provides strong motivation for pushing the state of the art further.

---

[1] [5, p. 311]

1.2 Learning Concepts from Examples

A *concept* is a rule that partitions a domain of instances into those instances that satisfy the rule, and those that do not.[2] For example, the concept of a prime number is a partition of the set of numbers into those that are prime and those that are not. The classification rule is:

x is prime if and only if x is an integer and x is evenly divisible only by x and 1.

A classification rule is a form of set description. Hereafter, the terms "classification rule", "concept description", and "set description" are used synonymously.

It is useful to view concepts as sets [4] because the calculus of set theory is then immediately available for manipulating and reasoning about concepts. Because there is no restriction on set constituency, there is no restriction on the universe of concepts. For example, the concept "threading a needle" can be described as the set of event sequences that result in a threaded needle.

In the paradigm of learning from examples, a learning program is shown known examples and counterexamples of the target concept. The *target concept* is the one concept that correctly classifies all the instances in the domain. Examples of the target concept are labeled *positive* instances. Conversely, counterexamples of the target concept are labeled *negative* instances. An instance that has been considered by the learning algorithm is called a *training* instance or an *observed* instance. If a classification rule is true for all observed positive instances and is false for all observed negative instances, then the concept that corresponds to the classification rule is *consistent* with the observed data.

The primary objective of the concept learner is to infer a classification rule that describes the target concept. While attempting to achieve the primary objective, the secondary objective is to infer a classification rule that is as close as possible to the target concept. As illustrated in figure 1.1, concept A is *closer* to the target concept T than concept B if and only if A classifies more instances as would T than does B.

---

[2] Webster's Dictionary [11, p. 293] defines a concept as "an idea or thought, especially a generalized idea of a class of objects".

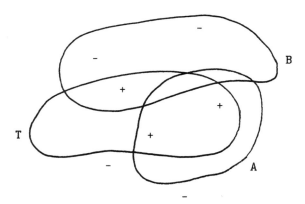

Figure 1.1: Concept *A* Closer than *B*

For a domain of instances I, there are $2^{|I|}$ distinct subsets over I. The domain I may be infinitely large, in which case the set of $2^{|I|}$ distinct concepts is also infinitely large. The set of all subsets over a domain I is the set of *all distinct concepts* over I. If two distinct concept descriptions each refer to the identical set of instances, then those descriptions are *synonyms*

The problem of inductively inferring a concept, based on observation of positive and negative training instances, is classic. Mechanical approaches cast inductive inference as a search problem [35]. Such a mechanical approach includes the following four steps:

1. Define a space of instances over which a concept is to be learned.

2. Define a space of concepts over the space of instances that can be searched mechanically. Each concept can be considered a hypothesis of the target concept to be learned.

3. Define an algorithm that searches the space of concepts. The objective of the algorithm is to identify the target concept T or some close T' as quickly as possible.

4. Deliver training instances for observation by the algorithm.

The fundamental characteristic of induction is that the target concept T is not known to the concept learner. Because T is unknown, there is no way to compare a hypothesis H to T. How can an H_i be selected as closer to T than some other H_j? The training instances permit pruning of inconsistent hypotheses; an inconsistent hypotheses cannot be the target concept. For the remaining consistent hypotheses, the question remains. Beyond consistency, hypothesis selection (induction) is guesswork. If making good guesses were impossible, the problem would be of little interest. Fortunately, humans regularly exhibit skill at inductive inference, so there is proof that useful inductive inference is indeed possible.

In the terminology of Artificial Intelligence, learning concepts from examples is a heuristic search for a best classifier of instances. In nontechnical terms, preference for one consistent hypothesis to another is a result of bias.

1.3   Role of Bias in Concept Learning

Given a set of training instances, *bias* is the set of all factors that collectively influence hypothesis selection. These factors include the definition of the space of hypotheses and definition of the algorithm that searches the space of concept descriptions. Learning concepts from examples is depicted in figure 1.2 as a function of two arguments, the training instances, and the bias for hypothesis preference. Although a particular set of training instances influences hypothesis selection, the problem of selecting training instances has more to do with teaching than learning. Choice of a training set is not considered here. Rather, for any particular set of training instances, the bias guides the learner to choose a particular hypothesis.

A program that learns concepts from examples is successful only when it has a bias that guides it to make a satisfactory selection from among the available hypotheses. Without the bias, the program has no basis for selecting one hypothesis in favor of another. If the concept learner is to make choices on a non-random basis, then bias is necessary [33]. The very act of electing a hypothesis is equivalent to making an inductive leap because the concept learner guesses that the hypothesis correctly classifies all the instances in the domain. That is, the concept learner assumes that the current hypothesis is the target concept. Had the bias been different, yet the training instances the same, the learner would have elected a different

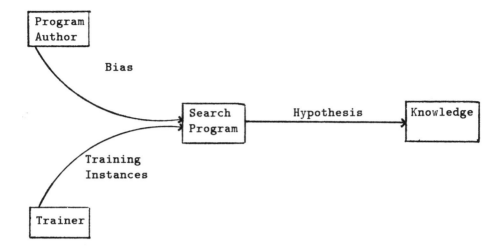

Figure 1.2: Role of Bias in Inductive Generalization

hypothesis. As a result the learner would have made a different inductive leap.

Two important features of bias are strength and correctness:

1. A *strong* bias is one that focuses the concept learner on a relatively small number of hypotheses. Conversely, a *weak* bias is one that allows the concept learner to consider a relatively large number of hypotheses.

2. A *correct* bias is one that allows the concept learner to elect the target concept. Conversely, an *incorrect* bias is one that does not allow the concept learner to elect the target concept.

The concept learner's task is simplest when bias is strongest and correct because the concept learner immediately elects the only choice available; the target concept. Conversely, the concept learner's task is most difficult when bias is weakest but incorrect because the concept learner cannot elect the target concept and has no other guidance regarding hypothesis selection.

To illustrate the role of bias, consider an example learning scenario. Person *A* is to learn a concept from instances presented by person *B*. Person

B only presents correctly classified positive and negative instances of the concept. It is the job of person A to infer the target concept that person B is endeavoring to teach. Person B presents the first instance:

(3,4) is a positive instance

Person A may perhaps form a hypothesis of the concept such as "an ordered pair of numbers". Person B then presents the second instance:

(6,5) is a negative instance

Person A may revise his hypothesis of the concept to be "an ordered pair of numbers in which the first is numerically less than the second". If person A has not made a random choice from among the set of distinct consistent hypotheses, then by definition he has been guided by bias to choose the "less than" hypothesis. Consider some alternative consistent hypotheses that A could have chosen instead:

1. An ordered pair of numbers in which the first is an odd integer.

2. An ordered pair of numbers in which the second is an even integer.

3. An ordered pair of numbers in which the first is an odd integer *and* the second is an even integer.

4. An ordered pair of numbers in which the first is an odd integer *or* the second is an even integer.

5. An ordered pair of numbers in which the binary sum has a 1 in the 4's place.

6. An ordered pair of numbers in which the decimal sum has a 0 in the 10's place.

7. A pair of numbers for which the sum is 7.

8. An ordered pair of numbers in which the second is one more than the first.

9. An ordered pair of numbers in which the first is not one more than the second.

Of note in the example is that the hypotheses make use of other concepts such as order, odd integer, even integer, logical "and", logical "or", logical "not", addition, binary notation, decimal notation, digit's place, and the "one more than" relation. These are terms that are commonly associated with numbers and logical combinations of features. There are other hypotheses that are consistent yet difficult to state succinctly, e.g. some apparently arbitrary set of pairs of numbers. If a person A is trying to infer a rule from examples presented by a person B, additional human factors come into play. For example, one assumes that there is a vocabulary of concepts that the people share. In addition, person A may try to guess what kind of concept person B would try to teach.

1.4   Kinds of Bias

Two major kinds of bias follow from the two major sources identified above. One source is the concept description language. The other source is the concept learning algorithm.

1. There can be a preference ordering (total or partial) over the hypotheses. For example, a relatively simple consistent description may be preferred to a less simple consistent description. Similarly, a consistent description that does not use a particular syntactic construct, e.g. $\vee$, may be preferred to a consistent description that does.

2. It is possible to restrict the space of hypotheses through which the concept learner conducts its search. By using a space in which not all hypotheses are represented, the concept learner is unable to elect hypotheses that are not in the space. Use of a restricted hypothesis space is a very practical method for focusing the concept learner on a set of preferred hypotheses.

It is of course possible to have hybrid forms of bias that come from both major sources. That is, there can be a preference ordering over a restricted space of concepts. Chapter 2 describes the biases that were employed in selected existing learning programs.

1.5   Origin of Bias

Because bias dictates how a preferred hypothesis is selected, based on given observed training instances, two critical questions arise:

1. From where does the initial bias originate?

2. How is misleading or inappropriate bias identified and changed?

The second question is the subject of the research reported here.

The research in inductive concept learning programs to date has contributed several good techniques for using a given bias to guide the way to choosing a hypothesis. These programs do not select the initial bias nor do they change the bias[3] during concept learning. The program author expends considerable time and effort searching for an appropriate bias that causes the program to perform well. As the author repeatedly shifts the bias and retests the learning program, a search for an appropriate bias is taking place. The human author uses both his experience with previous bias failures together with his knowledge as a domain expert to guide his search for a better bias. Bias A is *better* than bias B if the concepts inferred when using bias A are closer to the target concept than those inferred when using bias B. A bias is *appropriate* to the extent that the program author deems the resulting hypotheses inferred to be good classifiers.

The ability to search for an appropriate bias is a major skill that the researcher applies. As the researcher works on getting good performance from the learning program, he does part of the learning task himself by finding an appropriate bias. The thesis of the research reported here is:

1. Search for a better bias is a fundamental part of the learning task.

2. Search for a better bias can be mechanized.

An inductive concept learning program ought to conduct its own search for appropriate bias. Until programs have such capability, the search for appropriate bias will remain a manual task dependent on a human's ability to perform it. This gap in understanding constitutes the largest weakness in current methods for mechanical learning of concept from examples.

---

[3]with the exception of Waterman[62] and Lenat[22]

1.6   Learning to Learn

An inductive concept learning program that includes search for a better bias learns how to learn. A different bias changes not only what is to be induced in the current learning task, but also what is to be induced in subsequent learning tasks.

An open question is whether there are biases that are useful across many learning domains. For example, is a bias toward comparative simplicity generally useful? No such universally useful bias has yet been positively identified. The emphasis in the research reported here is on the ability to shift and therefore learn bias. Shift of bias is a less difficult problem because it is possible to observe search for and shift to a better bias. An interesting experiment (taking many years) would be to observe many cases of concept learning programs that shift bias, and then try to generalize on the properties of the biases that were selected. This is a possible approach toward identifying characteristics of bias, e.g. simplicity, that are useful in several domains.

1.7   The New-Term Problem

One kind of bias mentioned above in section 1.4 comes from the use of a restricted hypothesis space. A standard method for defining a restricted hypothesis space is to use a description language in which not all concepts are describable. If a concept is not describable in the description language, then it does not exist as a hypothesis in the hypothesis space. For example, a restricted description language might include a description for the concept of a prime number and yet not include any description for the concept of an odd integer. In such a case, the concept learner could elect the hypothesis "prime number" and could not elect the hypothesis "odd integer".

If the target concept is "odd integer" or if the concept "odd integer" is needed as part of a description of the target concept, then it must be made available to the concept learner. In the field of Artificial Intelligence, identifying a new concept and making it available to the concept learner is known as the *new-term problem*. If a new concept is added to the description language, the space of describable concepts has been changed. Because an incomplete description language contributes to or defines bias, changing the description language is equivalent to changing the bias. Thus, in the case of bias coming from a restricted hypothesis space, search for appropriate bias is equivalent to search for an appropriate description language. The problem of finding an appropriate description language is a classic problem in Artificial Intelligence. For problem solving programs, Amarel [1] shows how an appropriate representation simplifies the problem solving task. Concept learning is also simplified by an appropriate concept description language.

1.8   Guide to Remaining Chapters

Chapter 2 is a survey of selected learning programs. The objective is to identify the kind of bias that is used in each case. With two exceptions, Waterman and Lenat, the programs operate with a user supplied bias that remains static while the program attempts to learn. Lenat's EURISKO learns by discovery, not by example, but there are common issues regarding bias.

An approach to shifting bias is presented in Chapter 3. First, the problem of deciding *when* to shift bias is addressed. Following that, a three-step method, called the RTA Method (Recommend, Translate, Assimilate), is presented showing one approach for *how* to shift bias.

The RTA method is tested by building a program named STABB (Shift To A Better Bias) that provides an existing concept learning program LEX with the ability to change its bias. Chapter 4 describes the LEX program and the STABB program and shows how they fit together.

The STABB program consists of two procedures for shifting bias. Each procedure is an implementation of the RTA method presented in Chapter 3. The first, called "Least Disjunction", is the subject of Chapter 5. The second, called "Constraint Back-Propagation", is the subject of Chapter 6. Although both procedures use the RTA method, they differ sharply with respect to how they exploit available information.

Finally, Chapter 7 summarizes the research, lists the results, reviews the issues, and comments on directions for further work.

Chapter 2

Related Work

This chapter shows the role of bias in several well known learning programs. The first section includes those programs that do not change the bias during concept learning. The second section shows the only two programs known to the author that do change the bias during concept learning.

2.1 Learning Programs that use a Static Bias

The purpose of this section is to characterize several learning programs in a way that shows the kind of bias employed. All the programs use a single bias during the concept learning. Recall from section 1.3 that bias is the set of all factors that affect or define what a concept learning program will infer, given a set of training instances. Bias can be represented procedurally, declaratively, or both. Table 2.1 gives a set of definitions used below to characterize bias in the learning programs.

2.1.1 Vere's Thoth without Counterfactuals

Vere's learning program Thoth [59] searches within a restricted set of concept descriptions for maximally specific consistent hypotheses. Bias is instilled both by restricting the set of hypotheses that can be considered, and by preferring more specific descriptions to those that are more general. The hypothesis space is restricted by defining a description language in which not all concepts are describable. In particular, the description language excludes concepts that cannot be described as a conjunction of terms. Furthermore, only conjunctive terms (ground level or more general) explicitly defined in

h	The set of all possible distinct hypotheses over the domain of instances.
$res(x)$	A generic function that returns a proper subset of the set x.
$best(x, c)$	A generic function that returns a single element from the set x, based on criteria c.
TI^+	The set of observed positive training instances.
TI^-	The set of observed negative training instances.
TI	The set of observed positive and negative training instances.
$one(x)$	One element of x chosen at random.
$con(h, i)$	A function that returns the subset of hypotheses from h that are consistent with the instances i. It is assumed that the instances in i are labeled and are thus distinguishable as positive or negative.
$max(x)$	A function that returns the subset of maximally specific hypotheses from x.
$min(x)$	A function that returns the subset of maximally general hypotheses from x.
$cf(h, i)$	A function that returns a counterfactual description [60] that is consistent with the training instances i. A *counterfactual description* is of the form $A - B$, where A and B are each descriptions in h or are, in turn, counterfactual descriptions.

Table 2.1: Definitions for Characterizing Bias

the description language can be used in a concept description.

A characterization of the concepts inferred by the learning program is:

$$If\ (H' \leftarrow con(res(H), TI)$$
$$then\ max(H')$$
$$else\ \emptyset$$

The "*else* $\emptyset$" indicates that if the program cannot find a consistent hypothesis in the restricted hypothesis space, then it fails without finding any consistent hypothesis.

2.1.2 Vere's Thoth with Counterfactuals

Vere's learning program [60] searches within a restricted hypothesis space for maximally specific hypotheses that are consistent with the observed instances. If none can be found, the program does not halt with failure. Instead, the program commences a search for a description of the form $A - B$, which Vere calls a *counterfactual*, where A is a description that covers all the positive instances and some of the negative instances, and B is a description that covers those negative instances covered by A. The "$-$" is the set difference operator. "$A - B$" can be paraphrased as "$A \wedge \sim B$" or "A except B". In turn, to describe a given set of negative instances, it may be necessary to create yet another counterfactual description $B - C$, where B is a description that covers all the negative instances and some of the positive instances, and C is a description that covers the positive instances covered by B. The algorithm recursively reduces the problem of finding a consistent description in this manner until a nesting of set differences yields a consistent counterfactual description. Two counterfactual descriptions are shown in figure 2.1. The program halts with success when it finds a consistent counterfactual description.

If the program were to define the constructed counterfactual description as a new primitive, and add the new primitive to the restricted hypothesis space, then it would be adjusting its bias because the new primitive would become a member of the concept description language. By becoming part of the description language, the primitive would be considered prior to any attempts to construct new counterfactual descriptions.

A characterization of the concepts inferred by the learning program is:

$$If\ (H' \leftarrow con(res(H), TI)$$

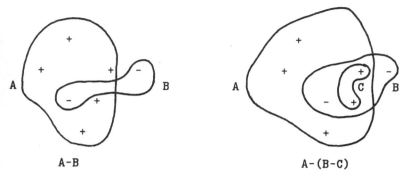

Figure 2.1: Two Counterfactual Descriptions

$$then\ max(H')$$
$$else\ best(cf(res(H), TI))$$

The "*else best*$(cf(res(H), TI))$" defines what is to be done when there is no consistent primitive description, causing H' to be empty. The bias is two-layered. First, the learning algorithm searches for a maximally specific consistent description within the restricted hypothesis space. If that search fails then a second search is conducted, this time for a counterfactual description. Vere's definition of "best" is based on the criterion of "equitable substitution", a particular strategy for deciding which variables to bind to which constants that was found by Vere to give "intuitively reasonable counterfactuals". Vere proves that a counterfactual description can always be found in the limit. This is a useful result but leaves two problems. First, the bias that comes from choosing a counterfactual may not lead to the desired inductive leap. Second, some concepts will never be inferred correctly. For example, assume that the set of all integers is describable and that any individual integer is describable. The concept of an even integer (each even integer is a positive instance of the concept and each odd integer is a negative instance) cannot be inferred by resorting to counterfactual descriptions. Each odd integer will need to be observed as a negative instance and there are infinitely many odd integers.

2.1.3   Mitchell's Candidate Elimination

Similar to Vere's Thoth, Mitchell's Candidate Elimination Algorithm [32] searches within a restricted set of descriptions, also called candidate descriptions. The difference between Mitchell's algorithm and Thoth without counterfactuals is that the Candidate Elimination Algorithm does not favor maximally specific consistent hypotheses. Instead, the algorithm stores *all* the consistent hypotheses that are within the restricted set of descriptions. This is made possible by noting that the consistent hypotheses are partially ordered by the subset relation. The algorithm stores the most general consistent hypotheses in a set named G. Similarly, the algorithm stores the most specific consistent hypotheses in a set named S. All other consistent hypotheses in the convex set need not be stored explicitly because they fall within the G and S boundaries. Space efficiency is improved by exploiting the order over the descriptions. This is analogous (in a totally ordered space) to storing all the numbers between a and b as the closed interval $[a, b]$. There is no need to list all the members that fall within the boundaries.

Bias comes only from restricting the set of hypotheses that can be considered. The restricted hypothesis space is defined by a restricted description language.

A characterization of concepts inferred by the learning algorithm (contained in the convex set $[G, S]$) is:

$$If\ (H' \leftarrow con(res(H), TI)$$
$$then\ [min(H'), max(H')]$$
$$else\ \emptyset$$

The "*else* $\emptyset$" indicates that if a consistent hypothesis cannot be found within the restricted set of hypotheses then the program fails. Note that the algorithm infers a set of consistent hypotheses, not necessarily a single hypothesis. Note also, that the characterization shows the effect of the algorithm, not the detailed mechanics.

2.1.4   Michalski's STAR Algorithm

In Michalski's STAR algorithm [29], a modified version of his A^q covering algorithm, bias is manifested in three ways:

1. A description language is used that is incomplete without allowing disjunction. Although disjunction is allowed, rendering the language complete, the rules (bias) for how and when to form disjunctions come into play only when a disjunction is necessary.

2. The STAR generator (hypothesis generator) applies specialization rules, e.g. adding conjuncts, to ensure that each hypothesis covers none of the negative instances. Hypotheses are then generalized, but without dropping conjuncts, to cover the greatest number of positive instances without covering any negative instances. The generalization and specialization steps are biased.

3. To choose among candidate descriptions from a star (set of hypotheses), user supplied preference criteria are applied, specified by the program's user as a "lexicographic evaluation function", abbreviated LEF. The description with the highest preference is selected.

If the chosen hypothesis does not cover all the positive instances then the hypothesis becomes a disjunct in a disjunctive description. Those positive instances that are covered are removed from further consideration and the algorithm is applied again to choose a hypothesis to describe the remaining positive instances. For each such repetition, the algorithm chooses a positive instance that was matched by as few descriptions in the most recent hypothesis as possible, thereby reducing the number of disjuncts needed in the disjunctive description.

The lexicographic evaluation function is a function that computes a value for a given description, based on specified weights for given features. The features can include simplicity, number of positive instances covered, expense of evaluating a description, and particular syntactic constructs that are believed to measure hypothesis quality [24, p. 356]. It is up to the user to decide whether the induced hypotheses are acceptable. If the user is unsatisfied with the results, then he tries again. Michalski points out:

> We disagree with many authors who seem to be searching for one universal criterion which should guide induction. Our position is that there are many dimensions, independent and interdependent, on which a hypothesis can be evaluated. The weight given to each dimension depends on the ultimate use of the hypothesis.

This indicates that a learning program would benefit from being told or being able to infer the ultimate use of the hypothesis. The bias of the learning system should be a function of or should agree with the ultimate use of the hypothesis.

A characterization of the inferred concept is $disj$ with $disj$ computed by the following algorithm:

$$p \leftarrow TI^+$$
$$disj \leftarrow \emptyset$$
$$while(p \neq \emptyset)$$
$$[\quad d \leftarrow best(con(res(H), one(p) \cup TI^-), LEF)$$
$$disj \leftarrow disj \cup d$$
$$p \leftarrow p - (d \cap p)$$
$$]$$
$$return(disj)$$

Note that there is always a consistent disjunctive description; the set of positive training instances. A misleading bias leads to election of an unpreferred hypothesis, not failure to select a consistent hypothesis.

2.2 Learning Programs that use a Dynamic Bias

Two programs that shift bias are known to the author. One is by Waterman, the other by Lenat. Because the bias is dynamic, it is more difficult to characterize than the above programs.

2.2.1 Waterman's Poker Player

Waterman's poker player [62] learns and refines a set of production rules that define a strategy for betting and playing the card game poker. The production rules are expressed using a description language that includes concepts that Waterman calls "heuristic definitions". A heuristic definition is a symbolic term that is associated with a discrete numeric interval, so that a continuous range of numeric values can be referenced by a single term, or concept. Consider an example production rule that was learned by the program:

If your hand is excellent and the opponent tends to be a conservative player and the opponent has just bet low, then bet low.

For each qualitative term, e.g. "excellent hand", "conservative player", "low bet", there is a heuristic definition that defines a mapping between the term and a continuous range of numeric values. For example, for the term "low bet", the associated values for the size of the bet range from 1 to 5. A heuristic definition allows description of a set of numbers by a single term. Because there is not a heuristic definition for each distinct subset of the numbers, nor for each distinct interval of the numbers, there is bias. The program can describe only those numeric intervals for which there are heuristic definitions.

Waterman's program learns in two ways. First, it is capable of modifying the domain of applicability of an existing production rule or of creating a new production rule. Note that the production rule mechanism used by Waterman, i.e. execute the first applicable rule, implicitly provides the ability to express counterfactual descriptions. A production rule that applies to situations to which at least one later production also applies, effectively has subtracted that much from the domain of applicability of the later rule. For example, assume there are two production rules

$$A \rightarrow B$$
$$C \rightarrow D$$

Due to the order of the rules, the second rule is equivalent to

$$(C - A) \rightarrow D$$

Second, and specific to the process of shifting bias, Waterman's program can adjust the heuristic definitions. For example, if training data show that the range of "good" extends too low, it can raise the lower limit of the range and thereby redefine the concept of "good". Shifting the boundaries of discrete intervals shifts the bias that the program uses. Note however that shifting a boundary of a numeric interval neither strengthens nor weakens bias, because it is equivalent to simultaneously removing an old description and adding a new description. The net number of available descriptions does not change. Waterman's program does not otherwise shift its bias.

2.2.2 Lenat's EURISKO

Lenat's EURISKO [21] learns by discovery rather than from examples. The goal of EURISKO is to discover interesting new concepts, not to induce a classification rule for a set of training instances.

EURISKO starts with an initial set of concepts, and then combines and composes them in various ways to produce new concepts. The program is driven by heuristics that define "interestingness". The program maintains an agenda of concepts to expand and explore ordered by an interestingness metric. That is, EURISKO *generates* a new concept or fills in an empty facet of an existing concept, and then *tests* the degree of interestingness of the new knowledge. New tasks associated with the new knowledge are inserted into the agenda based on the degree of interestingness. In this way, the most interesting avenues are selected and expanded first.

In the paradigm of learning concepts from examples, generation of new concepts that are then added to the available description language is a method of shifting bias, as suggested in section 1.7. When EURISKO generates new concepts however, it is not for the purpose of changing what it will induce based on a given set of training instances. Instead, EURISKO's generation of new concepts is for the purpose of testing whether combinations or compositions of existing concepts or functions produces something that qualifies as interesting. For EURISKO, there is no right or wrong, no induced classifications for training instances. Instead, there is a heuristic search that attempts to discover that which is interesting.

For EURISKO, creation of new concepts is not by itself a shift of bias. For EURISKO, the bias is the concept of interestingness. Apart from the initial concepts, it is the definition of interestingness that determines those directions that EURISKO will pursue. Unlike its predecessor AM, EURISKO can also operate on the concepts that define interestingness. That is, "interestingness" is itself a set of concepts that can be expanded and explored. As a result, EURISKO can shift its bias because it can learn and adjust the interestingness heuristics. An example from [22] shows how a new discovery heuristic can be added:

> If 2 slots (call them s1 and s2) of frame F can have the same type, then define a new heuristic, attached to F, that says: "If f is an interesting F, and its s1 and s2 are of the same type, then define and study the situation in which f's s1 and s2 values are equal."

By allowing the program to discover alternative definitions of "interestingness", Lenat allows the program to discover alternative definitions of bias.

EURISKO has a chance of discovering definitions of "interesting" that are better than the definition provided by the program author.

Chapter 3

Searching for a Better Bias

The problem of searching for a better bias, described in Chapter 1, is not yet well enough understood to be addressed comprehensively. To isolate a manageable research problem, it is necessary to make specific design choices and simplifications. Section 3.1 presents major design decisions, specifies the choices that were made, and discusses the reasons for those choices. Section 3.2 presents the RTA Method (Recommend, Translate, Assimilate) for shifting bias, which depends on the design choices outlined in section 3.1. The research is exploratory and can be characterized as an existence proof for demonstrating the thesis (page 9) subject to the specified simplifications.

3.1 Simplifications

This section presents five design issues for building a concept learning program that can shift its bias. The simplifications discussed here are fundamental to the RTA Method in section 3.2.

3.1.1 Original Bias

The problem of finding a good bias has two forms. First, there is the problem of determining the original bias that the program is to use. The *original bias* is the bias with which the program starts, prior to observing any training instances. The second problem is to find a better bias for the program to use upon deciding that the present bias is not good enough.

Choice 3.1 *Learn bias by shifting from one bias to another that is presumed to be better. Ignore the problem of determining an original bias.*

If a learning program can find its way to a good bias then choosing a good or bad starting point loses importance. One could start the learning program with an arbitrarily chosen bias and then let the program do the work of finding a good bias. The appropriateness of the original bias would affect the amount of training required by the learning program. With an abundant source of training instances, the extra time required by a suboptimal choice of the original bias may be entirely acceptable.

The author of a program that learns concepts from examples customarily provides an initial bias. A typical method is for the program author to consult authoritative sources (books or experts) who have previously defined useful concepts (a useful bias) in the domain. This is presently too difficult to mechanize. A less difficult problem is to recover from the inadequacy of a particular bias. The existing bias, the determination that it is inadequate, and the training instances observed so far all provide information that can be used to determine a better bias.

3.1.2   Representation of Bias

The method through which the bias is realized has a profound effect on the methods required to alter the bias or substitute a new bias. For example, if bias is encoded procedurally, then shift of bias requires procedure modification or generation. Similarly, if bias is encoded by a restricted description language, then shift of bias requires modification of the description language.

Choice 3.2 *Represent bias as a restricted hypothesis space, defined by an incomplete concept description language.*

A restricted space of hypotheses can be defined by a description language in which not all the distinct hypotheses are describable. A hypothesis space that does not include all distinct hypotheses is *incomplete*. Similarly, a description language in which not all distinct concepts are describable is also *incomplete*.

There are two major advantages in using an incomplete description language:

1. The problem of searching for appropriate bias becomes one of searching for an appropriate description language. A language that describes the

useful concepts in a domain is essential to forming a theory of that domain.

2. From a pragmatic view, a concept learning algorithm that represents bias in this way already exists. Mitchell's Candidate Elimination Algorithm [32] has the desirable characteristic that bias comes only from the restricted hypothesis space. Otherwise, the algorithm is unbiased because it does not choose a hypothesis from among those that are consistent with the observed training instances. Instead, the algorithm maintains the set of *all* consistent hypotheses (in the language) as the space of all candidate versions (called a *version space*) of the concept being learned.

3.1.3 Formalism for Description Language

A description language is expressed within a formalism. A *formalism* is a formal system in which a language is expressed. For example, a formal grammar of string substitution rules is a formalism for specifying a formal language. Another example, predicate calculus is a formalism for expressing well-formed formulae that represent theories. A theory can be used as a description (concept) of all that is true or false according to the theory.

Most formalisms have some kind of bias. Indeed, no formalism for a language of intentional descriptions has been identified as unbiased. The string formalisms are awkward for describing unordered objects, such as sets. The logic formalisms are awkward for describing ordered objects. Thus, the formalism makes the description of certain concepts impossible or difficult. It is assumed that each and every formalism carries with it some characteristic or implicit bias.

Within a formalism, bias can be represented explicitly by rules for constructing descriptions. The set of all descriptions that can be constructed using the rules is the *concept description language*. For example, if the chosen formalism is that of a formal context free language then the construction rules are the grammar rules and the concept description language is the set of all sentential and nonsentential forms that are derived through the rules from the distinguished start symbol. For a context free grammar, each rule shows how a nonterminal symbol can be specialized by replacing it with another string of symbols. If a description or sentence cannot be produced by some sequence of rules applications then the description is not in the language.

Choice 3.3 *Consider the problem of shifting bias within a formalism. Do not consider the problems of shifting formalism or identifying characteristic bias associated with any particular formalism.*

Change of formalism and understanding of characteristic bias implied by a formalism has received little study.

3.1.4 Strength of Bias

As mentioned in section 1.3, the extent to which a description language is restricted determines the strength of the bias. If a bias is strong and correct, then the concept learning task is relatively easy because the concept learner will be guided quickly to selecting the target concept. If the bias is strong and incorrect, then the concept learner may eliminate *all* hypotheses from the restricted space without finding the target concept. If a bias is weak, the concept learner may do little better than random selection of a hypothesis. Given some fixed number of training instances and some fixed amount of time, a bias that is too weak may prevent the concept learner from eliminating enough hypotheses from the space to be able to isolate a single hypothesis, e.g. the target concept.

Correctness of bias determines whether the concept learner is able to select the target concept as a hypothesis. Strength of bias determines how many hypotheses have been eliminated before observing *any* training instances. With no bias, there is no induction.

Choice 3.4 *Consider the problem of weakening a strong bias by adding new descriptions to the concept description language. Do not consider the problem of strengthening a weak bias by eliminating descriptions from the concept description language.*

The choice to design a method for weakening a strong bias is based on the view that learning is itself a process of ruling out some hypotheses in favor of others to be retained, e.g. Mitchell's Candidate Elimination Algorithm. If a bias is too weak, then the concept learner can, in theory, continue to observe training instances until the space of consistent hypotheses is sufficiently pruned. On the other hand, if a bias is incorrect and too strong, and the space of consistent hypotheses is emptied, the concept learner will not benefit from further training. The problem of an incorrect and overly strong bias is serious.[1]

A program author who designs a restricted hypothesis space characteristically errs toward defining a bias that is too strong because he includes in the hypothesis space only those concepts that he knows about and that he suspects may be useful in the domain. If the bias is incorrect, then the bias needs to be weakened in a controlled manner in an attempt to make the bias correct without making it too weak.

3.1.5   When to Shift to a Weaker Bias

In general, shifting to a weaker bias can be done whenever the concept learner decides that the existing bias is too strong or that a better bias can be identified. The decision to shift the bias is equivalent to choosing a new space of hypotheses to be considered. This is the same as a bias that calls for searching subspaces of all distinct hypotheses in a preferred order, i.e. a bias on shifting bias.

Choice 3.5 *Shift bias when the space of hypotheses being searched by the concept learner does not include a concept that is consistent with the observed training instances.*

It is assumed that the trainer correctly labels the training instances. Incorrect labeling is detected when an instance is classified as positive on one occasion and as negative on another. In such a case the two training instances can be discarded.

Using only the criterion in choice 3.5 enforces a single decision for when to shift bias. This is a fixed bias for when to shift bias.

3.2   The RTA Method for Shifting Bias

The objective of shifting to a weaker bias is to make it possible for the concept learner to elect a hypothesis that is consistent with the training

---

[1]like racism, sexism and other forms of prejudice

instances, and is as close to the target concept as possible. Because the concept learner cannot know which concept is the target concept, it is necessary to use heuristic methods for deciding exactly how to weaken the bias.

This section describes the RTA Method for shifting to a weaker bias. The Method is subject to the assumptions and simplifications described above in 3.1. The method consists of three steps:

1. *Recommend* (via heuristics) new concept descriptions to be added to the concept description language.

2. *Translate* the recommendations into new concept descriptions that are expressed in the formalism of the concept description language.

3. *Assimilate* newly formed concepts into the restricted space of hypotheses in a manner that maintains the organization of the hypothesis space.

Step 1 is for determining a weaker bias to which to shift. Steps 2 and 3 provide the mechanics for carrying out the shift. The resulting new concept description language is a superset of the former description language, providing a strictly weaker bias.

3.2.1   Recommending New Descriptions for a Weaker Bias

The first step of the RTA method is to identify a weaker bias to which to move. The approach used here is to add descriptions to the restricted hypothesis space, thereby weakening the bias. The task of step 1 is to formulate recommendations for new descriptions to be added to the space of hypotheses. The recommendations are then given as output to step 2. This section discusses how to identify a weaker bias to which to move.

The concept learner only shifts to a new bias when the existing hypothesis space no longer contains any consistent hypotheses. The knowledge that the existing description language contains no consistent descriptions shows that the existing bias is too strong. To alter the bias, new descriptive capability is added to the description language so that the new space of hypotheses contains at least one consistent hypothesis.

Figure 3.1 shows two partitions of the space of all distinct hypotheses. The first partition consists of two subsets; those descriptions that are in

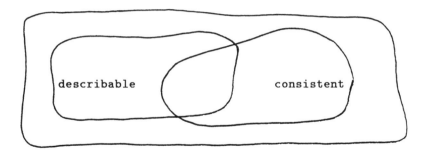

Figure 3.1: Partitions of the Space of All Distinct Hypotheses

the restricted space of hypotheses to be searched by the concept learner, and those that are not. The second partition also consists of two subsets, those descriptions that are consistent with the training instances and those that are not. As concept learning takes place, the new knowledge of the classification of the training instances allows the concept learner to identify inconsistent hypotheses. Thus, the set of hypotheses consistent with the training instances shrinks during concept learning. When the set of consistent hypotheses within the restricted space, i.e. the intersection, becomes empty, then a shift to a weaker bias is required. To weaken the bias, it is necessary to move the partition that defines the restricted hypothesis space so that there is again a non-empty set of consistent hypotheses within the now less restricted space of hypotheses. Thus, the set of describable hypotheses grows when the bias is weakened. Note that shift to a weaker bias is accomplished by enlarging the current concept description language.

Although the goal is to add consistent hypotheses to the restricted space, they are not to be chosen at random. Recall from section 1.3 that the selection of a hypothesis by the concept learner constitutes an inductive leap because the hypothesis specifies the classification of the unobserved instances. If consistent hypotheses were to be added to the hypothesis space without regard to how they classify unobserved instances, then there could be no confidence in the inductive leap when such a consistent hypothesis were selected.

The problem for the concept learner is to move to a new bias that will cause the concept learner to make satisfactory inductive leaps based on the observed data. Because the concept learner cannot already know which concept is the target concept, the concept learner must make an intelligent guess based on *heuristics* for shifting to a weaker bias.

The problem of selecting the initial bias is customarily solved by the researcher. Based on the experience of this author and several colleagues, the first choice for the bias will probably be incorrect. In the absence of a mechanism for selecting an initial bias, the problem of shifting to a better bias will remain important. The human researcher does a better job of choosing an appropriate bias on subsequent trials because he has learned something from the previous failures. Each time a bias fails, the researcher has new knowledge that he can apply in subsequent choices. The problem of shifting to a new bias differs from the problem of initially selecting a bias because one shifts to a different bias with the added knowledge. The learner has additional training instances and has a bias that has been judged unacceptable.

Consider an example heuristic that corresponds to Vere's counterfactual technique for constructing new descriptions:

> If the description language does not contain a consistent description then construct a new consistent description that is a counterfactual of existing descriptions.

The heuristic relies on existing descriptions in the restricted hypothesis space, the training instances, and the set difference operator "−" to determine the classifications of the unobserved instances. For example, one could define a new concept "negative number" as "a number that is not positive".

3.2.2 Translating Recommendations into New Concept Descriptions

The second step of the RTA Method is to translate the recommendations from step 1 into new descriptions within the formalism of the concept description language. The new descriptions are to be assimilated by step 3. This section discusses the need for translation and gives an example translation process.

The recommendations specify new descriptive capability to add to the description language. If a recommendation can specify something that should be describable then it is in some sense already describable. There are two kinds of learning however and each takes place in its own space. As per Bruner [4]:

1. *Concept acquisition* is accomplished by searching the hypothesis space represented by the concept description language.

2. *Concept formation* is accomplished by translating a recommendation from the space (language) of recommendations into a concept description that becomes part of the hypothesis space search during concept acquisition.

The recommendation language is used to specify new concepts that should be describable in the concept description language. A recommendation itself is not part of the description language because a recommendation corresponds to descriptive capability that is not yet in the existing concept description language. *Translation* is the process of identifying concepts expressible in the formalism of the concept description language that correspond to a given recommendation.

Again consider the counterfactual example. Suppose there is a recommendation to add a new concept "negative number" defined as "a number that is not positive". The recommendation may be of the form "add a new description N such that $N = R - P$", where R is the set of real numbers and P is the set of positive numbers. The description language may not contain the set difference operator "$-$". If "$-$" is not in the description language, then one or more translation steps could be used to remove it from the "$R - P$" part of the specification. One step could be to translate "$R - P$" to $R \cap \sim P$. A second step could be to evaluate $\sim P$ with a function that computes a complementary description within the formalism of the language. A third step could be to evaluate the intersection of "R" and the result of evaluating $\sim P$. By performing such translation steps, it is possible to compute descriptions that are expressed in the formalism of the description language. Translation of unusable knowledge into usable knowledge via equivalence maintaining transformations is an important problem also known as *operationalization* [38,39]. The task of re-expressing concepts is also being pursued by Keller [16].

3.2.3   Assimilating New Concepts into the Hypothesis Space

The final step of the RTA Method is to assimilate new descriptions into the space of hypotheses. The new descriptions result from the translation step described above.

The method calls for the concept learner to *assimilate* a new concept by adding it to the restricted space of hypotheses that is searched by the concept learner. The mechanics of assimilation depend on the organization of the hypothesis space. For example, if there is no organization, then assimilation is done simply by adding a new description to the set of available hypotheses. A second example, if the restricted space of hypotheses is partially ordered by the subset relation, then assimilation is done by defining new links between the new description and descriptions already in the hypothesis space.

Assimilation is essential because new descriptions must be made available to the concept learning program while maintaining the integrity of the existing organization. For any new concept, some change is necessary to the description language to make the new concept part of the description language.

There are two major problems.

1. *How* does one assimilate a new description? The mechanics depend on the formalism of the description language. For example, for a partially ordered space of descriptions, assimilating a new description corresponds to defining one or more new subset links between the new description and existing more general descriptions. That is, description x is assimilated as a specialization of existing description y by asserting that $x \subset y$.

2. *Where* in the description language does one assimilate a new description? This too depends on the organization of the hypothesis space. For example, for a partially ordered space of descriptions, deciding which sets are immediately more general than a new description is a non-trivial problem. Because a concept to be assimilated is not yet in the description language, one needs to be able to evaluate subset relationships based not on subset links and matching, but instead on the definition of the new concept.

As an example, consider the problem of assimilating a new description that originated from the construction of a counterfactual description. Assume that the space of hypotheses is organized by a partial order on the subset relation. How does one assimilate a new concept N defined as the set of negative numbers? Assume that the definition of N was derived through translation by evaluating $R - P$. Because it is known that $R - P \subseteq R$, N can be assimilated by asserting $N \subseteq R$.

Chapter 4

LEX and STABB

To experiment with the RTA Method (section 3.2), a program named STABB (Shift to a Better Bias) was implemented. Implementation is an effective discipline for testing ideas and for exposing unexpected problems. This chapter describes the learning program LEX[36] and shows how STABB has been made a subsystem of LEX. With STABB, LEX can shift its bias. Chapters 5 and 6 describe the two algorithms used by STABB, each employing the RTA Method.

4.1 LEX: A Program that Learns from Experimentation

LEX is a concept learning program that creates and refines heuristics that suggest whether a given operator should be applied to a given problem state in a forward-search problem solver. Associated with each operator, there is a heuristic that represents the concept "set of states to which this operator *should* be applied". The set of states to which an operator *should* be applied is a subset of the set of states to which the operator *could* be applied. The problem for the concept learner is to correctly determine the heuristics for each and every operator.

LEX learns heuristics in the domain of integral calculus. The program is initially given a set of problem solving operators. Each operator has a domain of states to which the operator can be applied, a rewrite rule, and a range of states that can be produced by application of the operator. For each operator, the domain of applicability describes states to which the operator *could* be applied. In contrast, for each heuristic, the domain of applicability

33

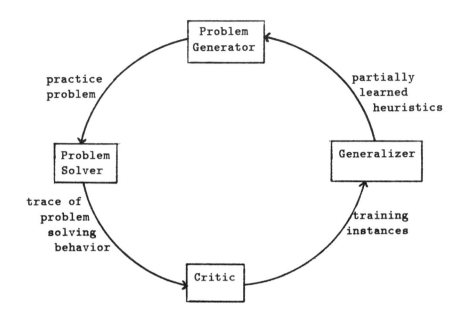

Figure 4.1: Top Level Flow of Control in LEX

describes states to which the associated operator *should* be applied.

As shown in figure 4.1, LEX is a system that generates problems, solves problems, criticizes solutions, and learns heuristics that guide the problem solver on future problems. Because the domain of a heuristic is a subset of the domain of the corresponding operators, the branching factor when using the heuristics is less than the branching factor when using the operators. Because fewer heuristics can be applied to a given state, fewer operators will be applied, wasting fewer search steps and thereby improving performance.

4.1.1 Problem Solver

The problem solver finds a solution using a modified uniform-cost search[42]. A goal state is one that contains no integral. When a state is produced for which a heuristic recommends an operator to apply next, the cost of the solution path to that state is discounted by as much as a factor of d. The cost of the path for the purpose of the uniform-cost search is based on the true cost of the path and the degree of match. The formula is:

$$cost(n) = truecost(n) \cdot (d - degreeofmatch) \div d$$

The d for LEX is 1.5. Note that if the degree of match is 0.0 then the discount factor is 1.0 and $cost(n) = truecost(n)$. When the degree of match is 1.0 the discount factor is 0.33. In this way, the heuristics directly affect the performance of the problem solver.

4.1.2 Critic

When a solution is found by the problem solver, the entire search graph is passed to the critic. Because the path cost may have been discounted during the uniform-cost search, the solution path is not guaranteed to be minimal with respect to true cost. For this reason, the critic calls the problem solver to expand those search paths that have a true cost less than the true cost of the solution path. If a cheaper solution path is found, it becomes the best solution path. Search continues either until all other paths have been found to be more expensive or until the resources allocated to the additional search have been expended. Given the resource limitation, it remains possible that the critic will not find the minimum true cost path.

The critic labels each operator application *along* the best found solution path as a *positive* instance showing a state to which the given operator should be applied. For each operator application that leads *away* from the best found solution path, the critic labels the operator application as a *negative* instance showing a state to which the given operator should not be applied.

4.1.3 Generalizer

The critic produces a set of training instances that are passed to the generalizer so that the generalizer can update the heuristics being learned for the operators. For each heuristic, the generalizer uses Mitchell's Candidate Elimination Algorithm[31,32] to maintain a version space of all candidate versions of the heuristic that have not been refuted.

The problem solver needs to compare a state and a heuristic that is represented as a version space. The comparison is made by evaluating the degree of match. The degree of match is estimated by computing the proportion of descriptions in the version space boundary sets that match the state.

4.1.4   Problem Generator

The problem generator is able to supply informative problems to the problem solver based on the current set of partially learned heuristics. The principal strategy is to generate a problem that is in the domain of two or more heuristics. When the problem solver determines which operator should have been applied, the heuristics will be modified through the learning process. The problem is informative because it will cause at least one heuristic to be modified.

The purpose of the problem generator is to automate the training function, so that LEX can propose, solve, and learn from problems entirely on its own. Alternatively, a person who wants to experiment with LEX can serve as the problem generator.

4.1.5   Description Language

Although LEX learns a heuristic for each operator, LEX has a single concept description language. In the one language, there is a need to be able to describe any heuristic that is to be learned.

LEX's description language uses the formalism of a context-free grammar. Customarily, grammars are used to specify a language of terminal sentences. As such, the set of all terminal strings defines the *instance language* or the set of all describable instances. To define the concept description language, *all* sentential forms, non-terminal or terminal serve as descriptions. A sentential form is the description for the set of all terminal sentential forms that it can derive in 0 or more steps. Note that this use of sentential forms as concept descriptions causes the desirable effect that a terminal sentential form is both an instance description and a set description that contains the single instance. The distinction between instance descriptions and concept descriptions is erased. For example, in the LEX grammar the non-terminal trig describes the set {sin, cos, tan, csc, sec, cot}, where each of sin, cos, tan, csc, sec, and cot is a terminal.

The complete LEX grammar is shown in figure 4.2. An explanation of the symbols used in the grammar is shown in tables 4.1 and 4.2. The grammar defines the concept description language which is the way that bias is represented for the Candidate Elimination Algorithm. Figure 4.3 shows four examples of integral expressions as they are represented within

LEX's description language.

There are three points to note regarding the grammar.

1. LEX uses a less familiar mathematical notation for function combinations. If $f(x) = g(x) \diamond h(x)$, where $\diamond$ is some combining operator, e.g. $+$, then one can[53, p. 32] also refer to the function using the combined name $g \diamond h$. For example, for $sin(x) + cos(x)$ would be written as $sin + cos(x)$. The representation using LEX's grammar is ((+ sin cos) x). This was done for simplicity so that the argument variable, in this case x, appears only once in the expression.

2. There are three descriptions afr, r, and knmz for which recognition predicates are defined. A *recognition predicate* is an algorithmic recognizer[13, sec 1.3] for the elements of a given set. The predicate returns **true** if and only if the argument is recognized as belonging to the given set. LEX uses selected recognition predicates for efficiency to take advantage of parsing already done by the LISP interpreter. Thus, the vocabulary of symbols consists of LISP atoms and parentheses, not single characters. For all x such that $recognitionpredicate(x)$, there is effectively a grammar rule $recognitionpredicate \rightarrow x$. In particular:

    (a) Something is an afr if and only if it is a non-numeric atom that is not used explicitly elsewhere in the grammar.

    (b) Something is an r if and only if it is a non-integer number or the atom e (Euler's constant).

    (c) Something is a knmz if and only if it is an integer that is neither 0 nor -1.

3. Any non-numeric symbol may have trailing digits appended to it. For example, the symbol sin can also be given as sin1. The digits are not part of the symbol as defined in the grammar. Instead, the digits simply make it possible to reference a particular symbol in an expression, e.g. (+ sin1 (* cos sin2)). LEX can observe or ignore such digits, depending on how it needs to use the expression. For example, when matching descriptions, LEX can ignore the digits. On the other hand, when rewriting a state, LEX can use the digits to ensure it operates on the intended symbols.

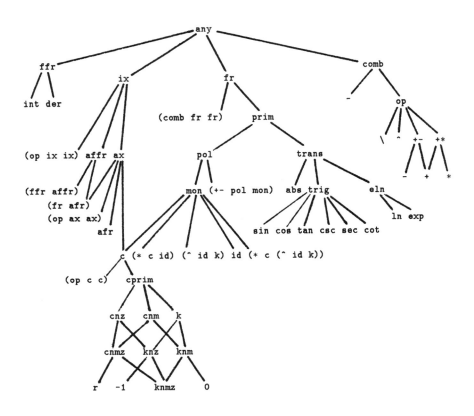

afr recognized as $\{x|atom(x)\wedge \sim numberp(x)\wedge \sim ingrammarp(x)\}$
r recognized as $\{x|(numberp(x)\wedge \sim integerp(x)) \vee eq(x,'e)\}$
knmz recognized as $\{x|integerp(x)\wedge \sim (x \in 0, -1)\}$

Figure 4.2: LEX Grammar for Integral Calculus

$$
\begin{array}{ll}
\int cos(x)dx & \texttt{(int (cos x))} \\
\int sin(x) + cos(x)dx & \texttt{(int ((+ sin cos) x))} \\
\int tan^2(x)dx & \texttt{(int ((\^{} tan 2) x))} \\
\int x \cdot e^x dx & \texttt{(int ((* id (\^{} e id)) x))}
\end{array}
$$

Figure 4.3: LEX Representation for Integral Calculus Expressions

abs	absolute value
affr	argument to a function of a function of a real
afr	argument to a function of a real
any	any legal expression or subexpression
ax	expression without integral or derivative
c	constant expression
cnm	real numbers except -1
cnmz	real numbers except 0 and -1
cnz	real numbers except 0
comb	combiner
cos	cosine
cot	cotangent
cprim	primitive constant, i.e. real number
csc	cosecant
der	derivative
eln	exponential or logarithmic
exp	exponential
id	identity function
int	$\int$
ix	expression with or without integral or derivative
ffr	function of a function of a real
fr	function of a real
k	integer
knm	integers except -1
knz	integers except 0
knmz	integers except 0 and -1
ln	natural log
mon	monomial
op	operator
pol	polynomial
prim	primitive function
r	real numbers except integers
sec	secant

Table 4.1: Grammar symbol interpretation for LEX

sin	sine
tan	tangent
trans	transcendental
trig	trigonometric function
\	division
^	exponentiation
-	subtraction
+	addition
~	function composition (tilde)
*	multiplication
+-	plus or minus
+*	plus or times

Table 4.2: Grammar symbol interpretation for LEX

This description language is based on standard classes of functions as presented in a freshman calculus book such as [53]. Through experience with LEX it became apparent that the language was not sufficiently rich to describe certain subclasses. The problem of language repair or augmentation became the subject of the research reported here. Experiments reported in sections 5 and 6 show examples of deficiencies and repairs, equivalently detection of incorrect bias and shift to a better bias.

4.1.6   Matching Two Descriptions

The ability to determine whether one description is more general than or equal to another is central to many concept learning algorithms. At a basic level is the classification task of determining whether an instance, a description of a singleton set, is included in a given concept. For many learning algorithms, there is a need to determine whether one concept, not necessarily a singleton set, is included in another. The Candidate Elimination Algorithm that LEX uses to maintain the version space for each heuristic specifically requires a Match predicate that tests the *moregeneralthan* relation.

For LEX, a description *a* is more general than or equal to a description *b* if and only if *a* grammatically derives *b* or *a* derives a sentential form within *b.* If description *a* derives *b*, then *a* matches *onto b.* If description *a* derives a sentential form within *b* that is a proper substring of *b*, then *a* matches *into b.* For matching, LEX uses a function *match(a, b, flags)* that returns a list of derivation trees showing how *a* matches *b.* If *a* is not more general than *b*, then the Match function returns a null list. The *flags* argument is not pertinent to the discussion here. A derivation tree returned by *match* is called a *map.* For example, cos is more general than (+ sin cos) because cos grammatically derives (in zero steps) the cos within (+ sin cos). A second example, trig is more general than (+ sin cos) in two ways. First, trig derives sin. Second, trig derives cos.

4.1.7   Operator Language

Each operator consists of the following set of items:

COMMENT   An English description of what the operator does.

LHS   A concept description for the domain of the operator.

RHS   A concept description for the range of the operator.

FORWARD   A LISP expression which, when evaluated, computes the values for all atoms in RHS that are not bound in LHS.

For each operator, its domain and its range are describable in the language. When the operator is applied, the LHS is first bound to the state. Then additional atoms, if any, are bound as defined in FORWARD. The bound values in LHS are available during this step. Last, the new state is produced by evaluating RHS under the bindings from the previous two steps.

Consider an example:

```
COMMENT   (* fr1 fr2) <=> fr3
LHS       (* fr1 fr2)
RHS       fr3
FORWARD   ((fr3 . [* fr1 fr2]))
```

The bracket notation used above in FORWARD indicates that the expression is to be evaluated if possible. For example, if fr1 and fr2 are each bound to a number then the multiplication can be performed. Otherwise an expression of the form (* fr1 fr2) is returned, using the bound values of fr1 and fr2. Note also the use of trailing digits on the fr symbols as described above in section 4.1.5. The 1 of fr1 is ignored for the purpose of matching but regarded when referencing bound values. If the operator were

$generalizer(insts)$
$\quad [\ while(insts \neq \emptyset)$
$\qquad [\ inst \leftarrow pop(insts)$
$\qquad\quad oldvs \leftarrow op_{vs}(inst)$
$\qquad\quad newvs \leftarrow CEA(inst, oldvs)$
$\qquad\quad op_{vs}(inst) \leftarrow newvs$
$\qquad]$
$\quad]$

Figure 4.4: LEX Generalizer without STABB

applied to (* 2 3) the result would be 6. If the operator were applied to
(* 2 sin) the result would be (* 2 sin).

Some operator applications require calculation of new values, as in the
above example, but others do not. An example of one that does not require
calculation is commutation, (* fr1 fr2) → (* fr2 fr1), because all symbols in the range are bound in the domain. In general, extra calculation is
necessary only when symbols are used in the range that are not bound in
the domain. The ability to provide each operator with a procedure for cal-
culating values to be used in the range gives the operator language the full
power of the LISP interpreter.

4.2 STABB: a Program that Shifts Bias

The STABB program shifts LEX's bias by modifying LEX's concept
description language. The control interface between LEX and STABB is
located entirely within the generalizer. Figure 4.4 shows LEX's generalizer
without STABB. Figure 4.5 shows the generalizer *with* STABB. CEA is the
Candidate Elimination Algorithm.

A characterization of LEX with STABB is:

If a version space is about to become empty (there is no consistent
description in the concept description language) then first change
the concept description language so that there is at least one
consistent description in the new language, then recompute the

```
generalizer(insts)
  [ while(insts ≠ ∅)
      [ inst ← pop(insts)
        oldvs ← op_vs(inst)
        while((newvs ← CEA(inst, oldvs)) = ∅)
          [ oldvs ← STABB(inst, oldvs, op, solutionpath)
          ]
        op_vs(inst) ← newvs
        push(op_oldinsts, inst)
      ]
  ]
```

Figure 4.5: LEX Generalizer with STABB

version space in the new language, and resume.[1]

The function STABB is shown in figure 4.6. Functions CBP (Constraint Back-Propagation) and LD (Least Disjunction) are the subjects of chapters 5 and 6.

In addition, the Constraint Back-Propagation routine requires application of operators in the backward direction to compute a constrained preimage. This is described in chapter 6 but is mentioned here to complete the discussion of interfacing LEX and STABB. Analogous to FORWARD, it is necessary to define BACKWARD.

---

[1] All version spaces computed in the old language need to be recomputed in the new language.

$STABB(newinst, oldvs, op, solutionpath)$
  $[\ if\ not(CBP(solutionpath))$
      $then\ LD(newinst, oldvs, op_{oldinsts})$
    $oldvs \leftarrow initvs(op)$
    $oldvs \leftarrow reprocess(op_{oldinsts})$
    $return(oldvs)$
  $]$

Figure 4.6: Top Level of STABB

Chapter 5

Least Disjunction

This chapter describes the Least Disjunction procedure of the STABB program that was described in Chapter 4. The procedure uses the RTA Method for shifting bias presented in Chapter 3. Two experiments with LEX and STABB show the procedure in action. Following those are a statement of the requirements for using the Least Disjunction procedure, an annotated trace of the procedure's activity during the first experiment, and a discussion of problems with possible solutions or directions for further work.

The Least Disjunction procedure uses the observed positive and negative training instances and the existing description language as inputs. The procedure *does not* make use of the learning goal[35], that is, it does not use the fact that the purpose of the learning is to find a domain of applicability for which each operator should be applied. The procedure only considers the observed instances as syntactic entities. As such, the method is *goal-free*. In contrast, the Constraint Back-Propagation procedure of Chapter 6 *does* make use of the learning goal, and is therefore *goal-sensitive*.

5.1 Procedure

The procedure shifts bias by adding a new concept description to the concept description language. The constructed description is equivalent to a least specific disjunctive description that is consistent with the training instances.

5.1.1   Recommend

The first step in shifting to an improved bias is to identify the new bias to which to move. To do this, a heuristic is employed:

If a new consistent description is needed, then construct a new description that is a least specific disjunction of existing descriptions.

The motivation for building a new description from existing descriptions is that the existing descriptions probably already describe concepts that are useful in the domain. The motivation for using a least specific (most general) form is that a new description will describe a useful class. A most specific form is unsatisfactory because it describes exactly the set of positive instances. Such a description corresponds to the inference that all unobserved instances are negative instances.

By defining a new description as a disjunction of existing descriptions, the classification information in the existing descriptions is incorporated into the new description. Vere uses this kind of heuristic for the purpose of inductive inference when he resorts to constructing counterfactual descriptions of the form $A - B$.

The Least Disjunction procedure calculates a specification of a new concept by searching for a least specific disjunction that is consistent with the training instances. A *least disjunction* is a disjunction of minimally specific descriptions in the language such that each disjunct covers as many positive instances as possible without covering any negative instances, and every positive instance is covered by at least one of the disjuncts. A least disjunction is computed in four steps.

1. Create an initial disjunctive description that is the set of positive training instances. The set of positive training instances is the most specific disjunctive description, and it is always consistent with the training instances, by definition.

2. Search for all generalizations of the disjuncts that produce descriptions that are more general than one or more of the positive training instances, but not more general than any of the negative instances. This generation step is done in a straightforward manner by efficient

generation of combinations of two or more disjuncts, coupled with early pruning of paths that produce inconsistent generalizations.

3. From the resulting list of generalizations (concept descriptions), eliminate any concept description that is more specific or equal to some other description in the list. The purpose of this step is to remove any description that is not needed in the disjunctive description being constructed.

4. Remove those embedding expressions of each disjunct that are identical for all the disjuncts. This step is necessary because all the disjuncts may share some single common context. To ensure that the disjunctive description under construction is as general as possible, it is essential that any such common context be discarded. The removal of such common context embodies a secondary heuristic:

> *If a concept is useful in one context, then it may also be useful in another context.*

The mechanism for doing this step is:

(a) Align the disjuncts according to how the domain of the operator matched each disjunctive term. For example, if trig matches (- sin cos) at sin and if trig matches (- tan cos) at tan, then the - are aligned, as are the cos. The context for each would be identical. If, on the other hand, the trig matched (- tan cos) at cos then the alignment would differ. The - of (- sin cos) would align with the tan of (- tan cos) and the contexts would be different.

(b) For each disjunct, delete all embedding expressions (common context) of the disjunct that occur identically in *all* the disjuncts.

For example, assume that the previous three steps produced a disjunctive description $\int x \cdot sin(x) \cdot dx \vee \int x \cdot cos(x) \cdot dx$ Then, in this step, the procedure would remove the common context $\int x \cdot \underline{\quad} (x) \cdot dx$ from each disjunct, leaving the less specific disjunction $sin \vee cos$.

5.1.2   Translate

The second step of the least disjunction procedure is to translate the disjunctive description, recommended by the first step, into a description using the formalism of the LEX description language. Specifically, it is necessary to create a new description that does not use the disjunction operator "$\vee$" required for describing a least disjunction. The procedure does this very simply by creating a new symbol for the vocabulary, and then defining the new symbol as more general than each of the disjuncts in the disjunctive description. In the LEX grammar, this step corresponds to creating a new symbol c, and then, for each disjunct d_i in the least disjunction, adding a new grammar rule $c \rightarrow d_i$ to the grammar that defines the concept description language. For example, to translate the new description $sin \vee cos$, the procedure could create a new symbol, $N16S$ say, and then add two new grammar rules $N16S \rightarrow sin$ and $N16S \rightarrow cos$. As a result of translation, the new concept is describable without explicit disjunction because the disjunction is implicit in the grammar rules.

5.1.3   Assimilate

The third step of the least disjunction procedure is to assimilate new descriptions, created by the second step, into the LEX description language. During the translation step, a new description c was created by defining grammar rules from c to other descriptions in the concept description language. The new description c is not yet part of the description language however because c itself is not yet derivable in the grammar.

The least disjunction procedure assimilates a new description c in two steps:

1. Define a set of descriptions mg that consists of the most specific descriptions in the description language that are more general than all the disjuncts used to define the new concept c. Each such description must include at least one negative instance because otherwise a consistent description would already have existed and it did not. The objective is to splice the new description into the description language. For example, in the case of $sin \vee cos$ and the LEX concept description language, the set mg is $\{trig\}$.

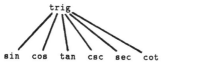 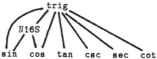

Figure 5.1: Bias before and after shift

2. For each description mg_i, add a new grammar rule $mg_i \to c$ to the grammar. For example, as shown in figure 5.1, when mg is $\{trig\}$, assimilation is completed by adding the grammar rule $trig \to N16S$.

5.2 Requirements

To guarantee that the least disjunction method can construct and assimilate a new concept description, three conditions must be met:

1. Every concept containing exactly one instance must be in the concept description language. This ensures that it is always possible to construct a consistent disjunctive description.

2. The concept containing every instance must be in the description language. This ensures that there will always be description that is more general than any constructed disjunctive description.

3. There must be a method for asserting that one description is a subset of another. This is necessary so that a new description can be assimilated by inserting it at the proper point in the concept description language.

5.3 Experiments

This section reports two experiments with STABB's Least Disjunction procedure that show how it shifted LEX's bias. Throughout this section, mathematical expressions are shown in standard Leibniz notation. In section 5.4 below, the program trace shows descriptions in LEX notation.

5.3.1 Experiment #1

In this experiment, LEX was given three problems:

1. $\int x \cdot sin(x) \cdot dx$

2. $\int x \cdot cos(x) \cdot dx$

3. $\int x \cdot tan(x) \cdot dx$

The first problem was solved in the following manner:

$$\int x \cdot sin(x) \cdot dx; u = x; dv = sin(x) \cdot dx \tag{5.1}$$

Applying op12, $\int u \cdot dv \rightarrow u \cdot v - \int v \cdot du$, produced

$$- x \cdot cos(x) - \int -cos(x) \cdot dx \tag{5.2}$$

Applying op3, $\int c \cdot f(x) \cdot dx \rightarrow c \cdot \int f(x) \cdot dx$, produced

$$- x \cdot cos(x) + \int cos(x) \cdot dx \tag{5.3}$$

Applying op10 $\int cos(x) \cdot dx \rightarrow sin(x)$ produced

$$- x \cdot cos(x) + sin(x) \tag{5.4}$$

The LEX operators do not add the constant of integration c.

The generalizer then refined the heuristic for op12, integration-by-parts, by using $\int x \cdot sin(x) \cdot dx$ as a positive instance. The resulting version space was:

G: $\{\int f(x) \cdot g(x) \cdot dx; u = f(x); dv = g(x) \cdot dx\}$
S: $\{\int x \cdot sin(x) \cdot dx; u = x; dv = sin(x) \cdot dx\}$

Recall from section 2.1.3 that a version space is a space-efficient representation of all descriptions in the description language that are consistent with the training instances. All that needs to be stored explicitly is the set G of most general consistent descriptions, and the set S of most specific consistent descriptions. All other consistent descriptions are stored implicitly between the boundaries.

LEX solved the second problem, $\int x \cdot cos(x) \cdot dx$, also by starting with op12. LEX's generalizer updated the version space for op12 to be:

G: $\{\int f(x) \cdot g(x) \cdot dx; u = f(x); dv = g(x) \cdot dx\}$
S: $\{\int x \cdot trig(x) \cdot dx; u = x; dv = trig(x) \cdot dx\}$

Recall that for LEX, the description *trig* describes the set:

$$\{sin, cos, tan, csc, sec, cot\}$$

When LEX tackled the third problem $\int x \cdot tan(x) \cdot dx$, LEX tried to use the integration-by-parts approach as it did for the first two problems, but it did not work. As a result, the critic identified use of op12 on the state $\int x \cdot tan(x) \cdot dx$ as a negative instance. The bias in the existing language prohibited the generalizer from finding a consistent description that could include *sin* and *cos*, yet exclude *tan*. Accordingly, STABB was called to shift LEX's bias.

The control strategy of STABB is to first try the Constraint Back-Propagation procedure described below in section 6. That procedure does not always produce a recommendation, the reasons for which are discussed in section 6. If Constraint Back-Propagation does not recommend a shift, then STABB tries the Least Disjunction procedure which, for the LEX concept description language, can always recommend a new consistent description. In this experiment, the Constraint Back-Propagation procedure did not produce a recommendation for a shift, so STABB used the Least Disjunction procedure.

The Least Disjunction procedure took the following steps:

1. Recommend that a description equivalent to $sin \vee cos$ be added to the description language.

2. Translate the recommendation, that $sin \vee cos$ be describable, into a new description $N16S$ defined as being more general than sin and cos.

3. Assimilate the new concept $N16S$ as more specific than *trig*.

Figure 5.1 shows the relevant portion of LEX's description language before and after the shift to the weaker bias. Following the shift, LEX reinitialized the version space for op12, and then reprocessed the training instances. After reprocessing the training instances, the version space for op12 was

G: $\{\int f(x) \cdot N16S(x) \cdot dx; u = f(x); dv = N16S(x) \cdot dx\}$
S: $\{\int x \cdot N16S(x) \cdot dx; u = x; dv = N16S(x) \cdot dx\}$

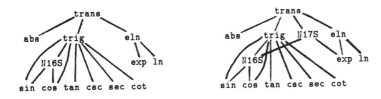

Figure 5.2: Bias before and after second shift

5.3.2   Experiment #2

In this experiment, LEX was presented with the problem $\int x \cdot exp(x) \cdot dx$. This experiment immediately followed experiment #1 described above. LEX found that the solution sequence from experiment #1 worked for this problem as well, and the critic gave the instance to the generalizer as a positive instance for op12. The description N16S does not include exp, and no description that includes exp also excludes tan, so LEX invoked STABB to alter the concept description language.

The Least Disjunction procedure took the following steps:

1. Recommend that a description equivalent to $N16S \vee exp$ be added to the description language.

2. Translate the recommendation, that $N16S \vee exp$ be describable, into a new description $N17S$ defined as being more general than $N16S$ and exp.

3. Assimilate the new concept $N17S$ as more specific than $trans$.

The changed portion of the concept description language is shown in figure 5.2. Following the shift, LEX reinitialized the version space for op12, and then reprocessed the training instances. After reprocessing the training instances, the version space for op12 was

$$\text{G:} \quad \{\int f(x) \cdot N17S(x) \cdot dx; u = f(x); dv = N17S(x) \cdot dx\}$$
$$\text{S:} \quad \{\int x \cdot N17S(x) \cdot dx; u = x; dv = N17S(x) \cdot dx\}$$

Note that the heuristic for op12 no longer needs the description $N16S$. The problem of superseded descriptions is discussed below in section 5.5.2.

5.4   Example Trace

This section shows an annotated trace of the LEX generalizer and STABB from experiment #1. To focus on the activity of the LEX generalizer with STABB, the problem solver and critic were bypassed. Instead, all three training instances were given directly to the generalizer.

Lines printed by the program are shown in small teletype font.

```
*(generalizer \plus-instances \neg-instances]

GENERALIZER receives 2 positive and 1 negative instances.

Processing positive instance for H1-USE-OP12.
```

H1-USE-OP12 is the name of the heuristic that recommends when to use operator OP12.

```
Apply OP12 to state #N
   State #N:
                (INT ((* ID SIN) X))
   Bindings:    ((INT1 . INT) (*1 . *)
                (FR1 . ID) (FR2 . SIN) (AFR1 . X))
```

N is normally the number of the node but is meaningless here because the problem solver was skipped. Recall that non-numeric atoms can have trailing identifier digits. The "1" in "*1" is such a digit, not a numeric operand.

A description used in a heuristic is referred to as an *hdscr* and is of the form (pattern bindings) where *pattern* is a description from description language, and *bindings* shows how the terms in the domain of the operator bind to values in the state that it matched.

The domain for op12 is (INT1 ((*1 FR1 FR2) AFR1)).

```
Version space initialized for H1-USE-OP12.


----- Heuristic H1-USE-OP12 -----

   If part of the state is of the form H1-USE-OP12
      then apply operator OP12.
```

```
OP12: INTudv => uv-INTvdu, u=fr1,dv=fr2dx
```

After 1 training instance, version spaces for H1-USE-OP12 are:

This is a version space, as defined by the G and S boundary sets. The boundary sets are not printed inside {} or (), the elements are simply listed down the page. The 0 0 is irrelevant here.

```
Gs:  O  O  (INT1 ((*1 FR1 FR2) AFR1))
              ((INT1 . INT1) (*1 . *1)
               (FR1 . FR1) (FR2 . FR2) (AFR1 . AFR1))

Ss:  O  O  (INT ((* ID SIN) X))
              ((INT1 . INT) (*1 . *)
               (FR1 . ID) (FR2 . SIN) (AFR1 . X))
```

Processing positive instance for H1-USE-OP12.

```
  Apply OP12 to state #N
    State #N:
                (INT ((* ID COS) X))
    Bindings:   ((INT1 . INT) (*1 . *)
                 (FR1 . ID) (FR2 . COS) (AFR1 . X))
```

Updating S#0; 1 description in the revised S.

```
----- Heuristic H1-USE-OP12 -----

  If part of the state is of the form H1-USE-OP12
    then apply operator OP12.

  OP12: INTudv => uv-INTvdu, u=fr1,dv=fr2dx
```

After 2 training instances, version spaces for H1-USE-OP12 are:

```
Gs:  O  O  (INT1 ((*1 FR1 FR2) AFR1))
              ((INT1 . INT1) (*1 . *1)
               (FR1 . FR1) (FR2 . FR2) (AFR1 . AFR1))

Ss:  O  O  (INT1 ((*1 ID1 TRIG1) X1))
              ((INT1 . INT1) (*1 . *1)
               (FR1 . ID1) (FR2 . TRIG1) (AFR1 . X1))
```

Note that COS and SIN have been generalized to TRIG in the S boundary set.

`Processing negative instance for H1-USE-OP12.`

```
  Do not apply OP12 to state #N
    State #N:
                (INT ((* ID TAN) X))
    Bindings:   ((INT1 . INT) (*1 . *)
                (FR1 . ID) (FR2 . TAN) (AFR1 . X))
```

`Updating G#0; negative instance inconsistent for H1-USE-OP12.`

Without STABB, LEX would not find a consistent description. Now LEX calls STABB to shift the bias.

`Attempting revision of CDL using constraint-propagation.`

CDL abbreviates Concept Description Language. Constraint Back-Propagation is explained below in chapter 6. It did not work here because the backward operator for op12 was never defined.

`Constraint-propagation returns empty-set.`

`Attempting revision of CDL using least-disjunction.`

The Least Disjunction procedure computes a consistent disjunction. An hdescr is a description that is used in a heuristic. An hdescr is of the form (description bindings). In this case, the hdescrs are exactly the positive instances.

```
Least disjunction hdescrs are:
  (INT ((* ID SIN) X))
    ((INT1 . INT) (*1 . *)
     (FR1 . ID) (FR2 . SIN) (AFR1 . X))
  (INT ((* ID COS) X))
    ((INT1 . INT) (*1 . *)
     (FR1 . ID) (FR2 . COS) (AFR1 . X))

Negative instances hdescrs are:
  (INT ((* ID TAN) X))
    ((INT1 . INT) (*1 . *)
     (FR1 . ID) (FR2 . TAN) (AFR1 . X))
```

The Least Disjunction procedure throws away common context of the descriptions so that the disjunctive description is more general.

```
Extracted disjunction is:
  (SIN COS)
```

Now, for assimilation, the least disjunction procedure identifies the most specific descriptions in the language that are more general than SIN and COS.

```
More general existing terms are:
  (TRIG)
```

The procedure changes the concept description language by adding new grammar rules. Every expression in the grammar is marked with either PAT or FUN to indicate to the matcher whether the expression is a pattern or a recognition predicate.

```
  Adding grammar rule to CDL:
    (PAT . TRIG) ==> (PAT . N16S)
  Adding grammar rule to CDL:
    (PAT . N16S) ==> (PAT . SIN)
  Adding grammar rule to CDL:
    (PAT . N16S) ==> (PAT . COS)

Least-disjunction was successful.

CDL revised, will reprocess all
     training instances for this heuristic.
```

The version space for H1-USE-OP12 is reset (to the starting condition where no training instances have been processed), and the instances are reprocessed. This is discussed below in section 5.5.1.

```
Processing saved negative instance for H1-USE-OP12.

  Do not apply OP12 to state #N
    State #N:
                (INT ((* ID TAN) X))
    Bindings:   ((INT1 . INT) (*1 . *)
                 (FR1 . ID) (FR2 . TAN) (AFR1 . X))

Saving instance until H1-USE-OP12 has been initialized.
```

It happens that the first training instance is negative. For LEX, version space boundary sets can be defined only after the first positive instance has been received. This problem could be circumvented if the description language contained a description of the empty set. If the S boundary set were initially the empty set, then any other description in the language would be more general. For historical reasons however, LEX simply saves negative instances until the first positive instance appears. At that time, the version space is initialized by defining the S boundary as the single positive instances, and by defining the G boundary as the LHS (page 41) of the associated operator. Then all saved instances are processed.

`Processing saved positive instance for H1-USE-OP12.`

```
    Apply OP12 to state #N
      State #N:
                  (INT ((* ID COS) X))
      Bindings:   ((INT1 . INT) (*1 . *)
                  (FR1 . ID) (FR2 . COS) (AFR1 . X))
```

`Version space initialized for H1-USE-OP12.`

The version space is initialized (again) because STABB reset it after changing the description language.

`----- Heuristic H1-USE-OP12 -----`

```
    If part of the state is of the form H1-USE-OP12
       then apply operator OP12.

    OP12: INTudv => uv-INTvdu, u=fr1,dv=fr2dx
```

`After 1 training instance, version spaces for H1-USE-OP12 are:`

```
    Gs:  O  O  (INT1 ((*1 FR1 FR2) AFR1))
               ((INT1 . INT1) (*1 . *1)
               (FR1 . FR1) (FR2 . FR2) (AFR1 . AFR1))

    Ss:  O  O  (INT ((* ID COS) X))
               ((INT1 . INT) (*1 . *)
               (FR1 . ID) (FR2 . COS) (AFR1 . X))
```

The version space for H1-USE-OP12 was initialized on a positive instance, so the saved negative instance is now processed.

```
Processing saved negative instance for H1-USE-OP12.

  Do not apply OP12 to state #N
    State #N:
                (INT ((* ID TAN) X))
    Bindings:   ((INT1 . INT) (*1 . *)
                (FR1 . ID) (FR2 . TAN) (AFR1 . X))

  Updating G#0; 1 description in the revised G.
  Optimal tradeoff for this G:
    Reject 0 positive and 0 negative instances.
```

The "optimal tradeoff" is not important here. It is part of the version space code that manipulates multiple boundary sets. That capability was disabled in favor of STABB's modifying the concept description language. No instances are rejected.

```
----- Heuristic H1-USE-OP12 -----

  If part of the state is of the form H1-USE-OP12
    then apply operator OP12.

  OP12: INTudv => uv-INTvdu, u=fr1,dv=fr2dx

After 2 training instances, version spaces for H1-USE-OP12 are:

  Gs:  0  0  (INT1 ((*1 FR1 N16S) AFR1))
                ((INT1 . INT1)
                (*1 . *1)
                (FR1 . FR1)
                (FR2 . N16S)
                (AFR1 . AFR1))

  Ss:  0  0  (INT ((* ID COS) X))
                ((INT1 . INT) (*1 . *)
                (FR1 . ID) (FR2 . COS) (AFR1 . X))
```

The new term N16S is used in the G boundary set.

```
Processing saved positive instance for H1-USE-OP12.

  Apply OP12 to state #N
```

```
State #N:
          (INT ((* ID SIN) X))
Bindings:  ((INT1 . INT) (*1 . *)
           (FR1 . ID) (FR2 . SIN) (AFR1 . X))
```

Updating S#0; 1 description in the revised S.

----- Heuristic H1-USE-OP12 -----

If part of the state is of the form H1-USE-OP12
   then apply operator OP12.

OP12: INTudv => uv-INTvdu, u=fr1,dv=fr2dx

After 3 training instances, version spaces for H1-USE-OP12 are:

```
Gs:  0  0  (INT1 ((*1 FR1 N16S) AFR1))
              ((INT1 . INT1)
              (*1 . *1)
              (FR1 . FR1)
              (FR2 . N16S)
              (AFR1 . AFR1))

Ss:  0  0  (INT1 ((*1 ID1 N16S1) X1))
              ((INT1 . INT1) (*1 . *1)
              (FR1 . ID1) (FR2 . N16S1) (AFR1 . X1))
```

The new term N16S is used in the S boundary set. Note that there is now a description in the language consistent with the three training instances. LEX, with the aid of STABB, handled the problem of shifting to a new bias on its own.

5.5 Discussion

Three problems surfaced during the experimentation. First, shift of description language may require recomputing version space boundaries in the new language. Second, descriptions created by the least disjunction procedure can become obsolete when superseded. Third, how does one choose among syntactic methods for shifting bias, e.g. least disjunction versus counterfactual?

5.5.1 Language Shift and Version Spaces

In general, it is necessary to adjust the version space boundary sets after shifting to a new bias. Recall that version space boundary sets are a compact representation of the set of all consistent hypotheses in the given description language. If the description language is enriched by adding new descriptions, the version space is *not* guaranteed to represent the set of *all* consistent hypotheses in the new language. It is only guaranteed to represent the set of all consistent hypotheses in the *old* language. There may be consistent descriptions in the enriched language that are incorrectly excluded from the version space that was calculated with the unenriched language. For this reason, it is necessary to compute a new version space in the enriched language. An obvious method, the one used by STABB, is to simply start over and reprocess all the training instances. No provably correct method for directly computing the new version space boundaries is currently known.

An important ramification of shifting the concept description language is that the version spaces for the other heuristics, computed in the old language, may be affected. Even though the version spaces for the other heuristics are not empty (i.e. there are consistent descriptions), shift of the language removes the guarantee that the version spaces contain all consistent descriptions describable in the language. Thus, it may be necessary to recompute the version spaces for *all* the heuristics. No method currently exists for checking whether, given a particular change to the description language and a particular pair of version space boundaries, the version space does in fact contain all consistent descriptions in the new language. STABB, as implemented, does not recompute version spaces in the new language for the other LEX heuristics, but should to be correct.

5.5.2 Obsolete Descriptions: Strengthening Bias

One problem that occurs with the least disjunction procedure is creation of descriptions that later become obsolete when they become known to be inconsistent with the positive or negative instances. For example, in experiment #2 in section 5.3.2 above, the creation of $N17S$ renders $N16S$, from experiment #1, unnecessary. That is, the original justification for creation of $N16S$, to be able to describe the heuristic for op12, is no longer present. This raises the problem of discarding obsolete descriptions, a form of strengthening bias. How does one identify a *stronger* bias to which to move? Three approaches are:

1. Keep track of *why* a description was created. For example, one could associate with $N16S$ the fact that it was created so that the heuristic for op12 was describable. If the justification for the existence of a description becomes invalid, in this case that $N16S$ ceases being used in the description of the heuristic for op12, one could then remove the description (assuming no other justification existed, e.g. the description is now in use in describing some other heuristic). Thus, when $N17S$ is created, and $N16S$ is no longer used to describe the heuristic for op12, the existence of $N16S$ would no longer be justified.

2. As suggested by Banerji[1], associate with each description the number of places in which it is used in all of the heuristics. A program could automatically discard descriptions that fall below a specified usage threshold. With a threshold of 0, the version spaces for the heuristics already do not use the description and are therefore correct in the current concept description language. If a concept is removed from the language while it is still in use in a heuristic, then there are two possibilities. First, the version spaces need to be recomputed and no version space becomes empty. Second, the version spaces need to be recomputed and a at least one becomes empty. The former case is acceptable but the latter is not. If a description is needed, even though it is not used much, do not remove it.

3. Conduct a search for candidate descriptions in the description language that can be removed from the language without causing any version space computed in such a language to be empty. For any single version space, this is uninteresting because any candidate description can be eliminated as easily as another. For multiple version spaces based on a single description language however, as in the case of LEX, the problem is interesting. One would attempt to search for a further restricted description language that would result in the overall smallest non-empty version spaces for all the heuristics.

---

[1] personal communication

5.5.3   Choosing Among Syntactic Methods

Why prefer one syntactic method to another? In experiment #1 above, a Vere's Counterfactual method could have recommended a new concept $trig \wedge \sim tan$. The Least Disjunction procedure recommended a new concept $sin \vee cos$. There is no apparent advantage to either one. Possibly, if the concept learner had some idea or clue about the syntactic properties of the target concept, then there might be a criterion for preferring one method to another, but such a criterion is extremely weak.

Descriptions that are not based on *why* an instance is either positive or negative do not capture the essence of a concept. A disjunctive description that is a list of disjoined positive instances does *not* describe why those instances are positive, only that they are. Similarly, neither does a counterfactual description that is a list of excepted negative instances describe why those instances are excepted, only that they are.

As an example, consider the problem of making the inductive leap that positive instances {2,4,6,8} and negative instances {1,3,5,7} are indicative of the set of even integers. Assume that there is a description for the set of integers, but no subclasses of integers. Consider four possible descriptions:

1. Syntactic via Disjunction: $2 \vee 4 \vee 6 \vee 8$

2. Syntactic via Counterfactual: $(((integers \wedge \sim 1) \wedge \sim 3) \wedge \sim 5) \wedge \sim 7$

3. Analytic via Division: $\{x | remainder(x, 2) = 0\}$

4. Analytic via Binary: $\{x | logicaland(x, 1) = 0\}$

Syntactic methods are useful because they can lead to descriptions of useful sets. A preferable approach, however, is to attempt to draw on information that can drive an analytic method. It is exactly this approach that is pursued in the next chapter.

Chapter 6

Constraint Back-Propagation

This chapter describes the Constraint Back-Propagation procedure [54,55] of the STABB program described in Chapter 4. The procedure uses the RTA Method for shifting bias. Three experiments with LEX and STABB show the procedure in action. Following those are a statement of the requirements for using the Constraint Back-Propagation procedure, an annotated trace of the procedure's activity during part of the first experiment, and a discussion of problems with possible solutions or directions for further work.

Unlike the Least Disjunction procedure in Chapter 5, Constraint Back-Propagation makes explicit use of the learning goal, that is, it takes advantage of the fact that the concepts to be learned describe when and when not to apply given operators. Instead of considering only the training instances and the description language, the procedure also uses a set of backward problem solving operators, a description of the set of solved problems, and the solution sequence from which the training instances were extracted, to help determine a shift to a new bias. As such, the method is *goal-sensitive*.

6.1 Procedure

When LEX cannot find a consistent description to describe the domain of a heuristic, instead of examining individual training instances, the Constraint Back-Propagation procedure analyzes the solution sequence, also known as the operator sequence, to determine how to adjust LEX's bias. The procedure shifts bias by adding one or more concept descriptions to the concept description language. Each constructed description describes a concept that is needed to describe the domain of the operator sequence. By deducing the domain of an operator sequence such that application of the operator sequence to a state in the domain will produce a solution, it is possible to identify useful new concepts to add to the description language.

6.1.1 Recommend

The first step in shifting to an improved bias is to identify the new bias to which to move. To do this, a heuristic is employed:

> *If an operator sequence leads to a solution, then deduce a new concept description that describes the domain of the operator sequence.*

This heuristic exploits the knowledge that the recommended domain of applicability for a given operator is the union of the domains of all useful operator sequences that start with the given operator. To describe the union, one can start by being able to describe the domain of one useful operator sequence.

To compute a specification of the domain of an operator sequence that produces a state in a given range, in this case the set of solved problems, a deduction procedure known as *goal regression*[61] is used. The goal concept is regressed backward through the operator sequence to deduce the domain of the sequence. Here, the procedure for regressing the goal is called *Constraint Back-Propagation*. It is used as a heuristic method for identifying new concepts that should be describable in the description language. The STRIPS program [10] computes preconditions for macrooperators by reasoning about constraints. Waldinger's program [61] for achieving simultaneous goals uses goal regression to deduce a restricted domain of an operator such that application of the operator to a state in the restricted domain is guaranteed to produce a state in an intended restricted range. Stallman and Sussman's EL [51] computes values at various points in electrical circuits by reasoning from known values, analogous to solving a system of simultaneous equations. Stefik's MOLGEN [52] plans experiments in molecular genetics. Whenever constraints become known or specialized during the planning process, actions that are inconsistent with the constraints are eliminated. The CRITTER program [17] uses constraint propagation to reason about digital circuits. From a statement of output specifications and definitions of components in a circuit, the program deduces input specifications of one component and propagates them backward through the rest of the components in the circuit. More recently, Minton has studied using goal regression to deduce winning game-playing strategies [30].

Constraint Back-Propagation is a procedure for deducing the domain of an operator sequence or macrooperator that produces a correctly constrained range of states. Such a constrained domain is also called the $preimage_{op_i}$[1] of the constrained range through the given operator and is defined formally as:

$$preimage_{op_i}(R) = \{d | op_i(d) \in R\}$$

The Constraint Back-Propagation procedure computes the following recurrence relation:

$$C_n = \{x | Goal(x)\}$$

$$C_{n-1} = preimage_{op_i}(intersect(range(op_i), C_n))$$

where $Goal(x)$ is true if x satisfies the goal. For LEX, the goal is to solve the integral, so a state satisfies the goal if does not contain an integral. For LEX, C_n is defined directly as ax in the LEX grammar. Op_i is the nth operator in the solution sequence.

By intersecting the set of all solved problems with the range of the operator, the procedure calculates the subset of the range containing solved problems. As shown in figure 6.1, by applying the operator to the subset in the backward direction, the procedure calculates the constrained domain (preimage) of the operator such that application of the operator to any state in the constrained domain produces a solved problem. The procedure computes the constrained domain of each previous tail of the sequence.

The Constraint Back-Propagation procedure uses backward operators, as opposed to strict inverse operators. An inverse operator, by definition, undoes the effect of the corresponding operator. An operator that is a one-one or one-many mapping has a functional inverse. An operator that is a many-one or many-many mapping does not have a functional inverse, because there is not a unique value in the domain that maps to the range. A backward operator differs from an inverse operator because it maps a set

---

[1]page 17 in [40]

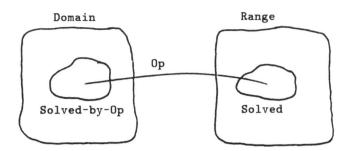

Figure 6.1: Constraint Back-Propagation

of states in the range to a *set* of states in the domain. Constraint Back-Propagation requires the ability to compute the preimage of a constrained range through a given operator. Constraint Back-Propagation does not require that operators be invertible.

As described in section 4.1.7, each LEX operator includes a LISP expression on the property FORWARD for computing any new values needed as part of the operator application. In every case, the expression for FORWARD is straightforward because the forward operators are written to map a single problem state in the domain of the operator to a single problem state in the range. For STABB, each operator can be modified to also include a LISP expression on the property BACKWARD for computing new values in the backward application of the operator. The BACKWARD expression is of a different nature because it can map a set of states in the range to a set of states in its domain. The LISP expression on BACKWARD must encode how to compute bound values for the domain (see section 4.1.7 for details on the mechanics of applying an operator). Consider three cases:

1. If no LISP evaluation is needed, as with commutation, (+ fr1 fr2)↔(+ fr2 fr1), then there will be no need to shift bias because any description in the range of the operator is immediately describable in the domain.

2. If LISP evaluation is required, but the result of applying the backward operator is a single state, then the state is already describable in the domain.

3. If LISP evaluation is required, and the result of applying the backward operator is a set of two or more states, then the operator calls a
   function named Lookup-or-Make. The Lookup-or-Make function constructs a recognition predicate, based on the LISP evaluation that is
   to be applied to the argument of the recognition predicate, and the
   constrained set in which the result must be included. If a recognition
   predicate based on these two arguments already exists, then the corresponding symbol in the description language is returned. If a such
   recognition predicate does not exist, it is created and associated with
   a new symbol, assimilated into the description language (described
   below in section 6.1.3), and the new symbol is returned.

Consider an example. There is an operator $op99\ c \rightarrow 2 \cdot (c \div 2)$, where
c is any real number. The procedure is given the task of propagating $2 \cdot k$
backward though op99, where k is the set of integers. The intersection of
$2 \cdot (c \div 2)$ and $2 \cdot k$ evaluates to $2 \cdot k$. Passing $2 \cdot k$ through $op99^{backward}$, the
constrained domain of the operator must be the set of numbers for which
each (number) is equivalent to 2 multiplied by some integer, i.e. the even
numbers. The set of even integers is, of course, a proper subset of the set of
real numbers. This illustration is continued below in the next two sections.

Although the three steps of the RTA Method are described here in turn,
the three steps are actually done for each operator as the constraints back
propagate through the solution sequence. That is, there can be a shift of
bias via recommendation, translation, and assimilation at each step in the
operator sequence.

6.1.2   Translate

The second step of the Constraint Back-Propagation procedure is to
translate the recommendations, produced by the first step, into descriptions
using the formalism of the LEX description language. *Expansion* of the
recurrence relation above over a given operator sequence provides a specification for a new concept description. *Evaluation* of the recurrence relation
translates the specification into a new concept description expressed in the
formalism of the concept description language. The specification uses the
terms $preimage()$, $intersect()$, and $op^{backward}()$. The new translated description does not.

The procedure depends on being able to evaluate the intersection of two descriptions, and on being able to apply a backward operator. Certain backward operators were difficult but not impossible to implement for LEX, e.g. the backward operator for integration-by-parts. Any time that intersection cannot be calculated or a backward operator cannot be applied, the procedure aborts in the translation step and therefore fails to complete the shift to a new bias. In such a case, STABB continues with the Least Disjunction procedure.

New descriptions are created during the translation process when necessary. For example, applying $op99^{backward}$ to $2 \cdot k$ requires creation of a description for the set of even integers. If the description of a constrained domain is computed by other than string transposition, e.g. multiplication, then the translation procedure constructs a new description in the form of a recognition predicate. Using the definition of preimage above, for some set D computed as $D = f^{backward}(R)$, the corresponding recognition predicate is $\{d|match(R, f(d))\}$. The predicate defines those elements to which one can apply the operation and produce a result that satisfies the constraint. For example, to describe the set in which each element is equivalent to $2 \cdot k$, for some k, the corresponding recognition predicate is $\{x|match('k, \lfloor x/2 \rfloor)\}$. The $'k$ is the symbol k in the LEX grammar for the set of integers. A new description is created by generating a new symbol NS for the vocabulary of the language, and then associating the definition of the new recognition predicate with the new symbol by adding a grammar rule of the form $NS \rightarrow new.recognition.predicate$.

Creation of a new definition for a recognition predicate does not necessarily mean that a new description will be incorporated into the concept description language. When a new definition is created, the translation algorithm (via Lookup-or-Make) first searches for a concept in the language with a syntactically equal definition. If one is found, the corresponding grammar symbol is returned. Because the procedure generates recognition predicates in only one way, any attempt to create a second syntactically identical definition will be prevented by this test.

In addition to application of backward operators, there is the problem of evaluating intersection of descriptions. This is done with the intersection function:

```
Intersection(x,y) =
 [ If Match(x,y)
    then y
    else
    If Match(y,x)
    then x
    else
    Most-General(
       Union(Intersection(Next-More-Specific(x),y),
             Intersection(x,Next-More-Specific(y))))
 ]
```

where Most-General is a function that returns the most general descriptions from its argument, and Next-More-Specific is a function that returns those descriptions in the language that are immediately more specific than the argument. When Intersection returns more than one description, then the intersection is the disjunction of those descriptions, and the disjunction is not describable in the description language. For example, Intersection(sin,(+ trig (+ ln fr))) returns (+ trig (+ ln sin)) $\vee$ (+ sin (+ ln fr)) due to the way in which *sin* can specialize (+ trig (+ ln fr)) at trig or fr. Disjunction is not a problem however, because the routines within the Least Disjunction procedure, section 5, can be called to translate and assimilate a disjunctive description.

6.1.3 Assimilate

The third step of the Constraint Back-Propagation procedure is to assimilate new descriptions, created by the second step, into the LEX description language. To assimilate a new description NS, the procedure must add the new description NS to the concept description language. Those concepts that are more specific than NS are well defined by the recognition predicate created during translation in step 2. The concept NS is not yet in the language however, because NS is not itself yet derivable in the grammar.

The Constraint Back-Propagation procedure assimilates a new description NS by adding a new grammar rule of the form $d \to NS$. The description d is the unconstrained description that was used in the domain of the corresponding operator. For example, for op99, the operator rewrites c as

$2 \cdot [c \div 2]$. When assimilating a new description for even integer, $N22S$ say the new grammar rule would be $c \rightarrow N22S$.

Using a description in an operator's domain as the generalization of the new description has two drawbacks.

1. Although the method does not incorrectly assert any subset relation it is nevertheless weak because it does not assert all correct subset re lations. For example, it is not incorrect to assert that the set of "even integers" is a specialization of the set of "real numbers", but the asser tion is weak because it does not tell the whole story. It would be much stronger to assert that the set of "even integers" is a specialization of the set of "integers".

2. The extent to which the operator is general is the extent to which the proper point of assimilation is poorly specified. A program autho will want to write operators in as general a form as possible so that no legal transformation is unnecessarily unavailable to the problem solver. Using this weak assimilation method however, the program author would want to write operators in as specific a form as possibl so that assimilation would be accurate.

In section 6.5.1 below, an alternative approach to assimilation is suggested that avoids these drawbacks.

6.2   Requirements

To guarantee that the Constraint Back-Propagation method can con struct and assimilate a new concept description, four conditions must be met:

1. A description of the set of solved states is needed so that the procedur can intersect the range of an operator with the set of solved states t compute the set of solved states that can be produced by the operato

2. A function to compute the intersection of two descriptions is necessar so that the range of an operator can be constrained as necessary. Th case of intersecting the range of an operator with the set of solve problems is necessary so that application of the backward operator t

the constrained range will lead to a constrained domain the describes the set of states "solved by application op_x".

3. For each operator, a definition of how to apply the operator in the backward direction to a set of states (compute the preimage) is needed so that a constrained domain can be calculated.

4. For any operator that includes arithmetic computation, or other kinds of computation not modeled in the grammar, it is necessary that such computations can be incorporated in a concept description. In the LEX grammar this is possible via recognition predicates.

6.3 Experiments

Three experiments are presented, each showing a case in which STABB's Constraint Back-Propagation procedure was invoked. The first experiment shows the creation of new descriptions and the resulting shift in bias. All three experiments expose issues that are given further consideration.

6.3.1 Experiment #1

In this experiment, LEX found a solution for $\int cos^7(x) \cdot dx$ as follows:

$$\int cos^7(x) \cdot dx \tag{6.5}$$

Applying op51, $f^c \rightarrow f^{[c-1]} \cdot f$ produced

$$\int cos^6(x) \cdot cos(x) \cdot dx \tag{6.6}$$

Applying op50, $f^c \rightarrow (f^2)^{[c/2]}$ produced

$$\int (cos^2(x))^3 \cdot cos(x) \cdot dx \tag{6.7}$$

Applying op52, $cos^2 \rightarrow 1 - sin^2$ produced

$$\int (1 - sin^2(x))^3 \cdot cos(x) \cdot dx \tag{6.8}$$

Applying op43, $\int f^c(g(x)) \cdot g'(x) \cdot dx \rightarrow \int f^c(u) \cdot du; u = g(x)$ produced

$$\int (1 - u^2)^3 \cdot du, u = sin(x) \tag{6.9}$$

At this point the polynomial can be multiplied, the integral of sums be rewritten as a sum of integrals, and each integral solved easily. LEX does not have a multiply-polynomial operator so the actual solution sequence from this point is bizarre. That is of no concern here.

LEX was then given $\int cos^6(x) \cdot dx$ for which the same solution failed. This was not a problem for LEX because the description 7 includes 7 and excludes 6. Finally, LEX was given $\int cos^5(x) \cdot dx$ for which the same solution worked. This was a problem because LEX's description language did not contain a description that included $\int cos^7(x) \cdot dx$ and $\int cos^5(x) \cdot dx$, yet excluded $\int cos^6(x) \cdot dx$. LEX called STABB to shift the bias so that the language could describe the instances. STABB tried the Constraint Back-Propagation procedure. The procedure ran into one representation problem that is discussed below. Otherwise the procedure proceeded as follows:

As discussed above, the last portion of the actual operator sequence is bizarre because LEX does not have a multiply-polynomial operator. The constraint in such an operator is that the exponent be an integer, so the propagation starts here with:

$$\int poly^k(u) \cdot du, u = f(x) \tag{6.10}$$

Intersecting the range of op43, $\int f^c(g(x)) \cdot g'(x) \cdot dx \rightarrow \int f^c(u) \cdot du; u = g(x)$, produces

$$\int poly^k(u) \cdot du, u = f(x)$$

Applying op43 in the backward direction produces

$$\int poly^k(f(x)) \cdot f'(x) \cdot dx \tag{6.11}$$

Intersecting the range of op52, $cos^2 \rightarrow 1 - sin^2$, produces

$$\int (1 - sin^2(x))^k \cdot cos(x) \cdot dx$$

Applying op52 in the backward direction produces

$$\int (cos^2(x))^k \cdot cos(x) \cdot dx \tag{6.12}$$

Intersecting the range of op50, $f^c \rightarrow (f^2)^{\lfloor c/2 \rfloor}$, produces

$$\int (cos^2(x))^{even/2} \cdot cos(x) \cdot dx$$

Applying op50 in the backward direction produces

$$\int cos^{even}(x) \cdot cos(x) \cdot dx \tag{6.13}$$

Intersecting the range of op51, $f^c \rightarrow f^{\lfloor c-1 \rfloor} \cdot f$, produces

$$\int cos^{odd-1}(x) \cdot cos(x) \cdot dx$$

Applying op51 in the backward direction produces

$$\int cos^{odd}(x) \cdot dx \tag{6.14}$$

The last two steps of the back propagation sequence (first two steps of solution sequence) are particularly noteworthy. For op50, the result of $\lfloor c/2 \rfloor$ must be in k forcing the creation of a new concept "those elements of c which when divided by 2 are constrained to be in k", otherwise known as the set of even integers. For op51, the result of $\lfloor c-1 \rfloor$ must be in *even* forcing the creation of a new concept "those elements of c which when decremented by 1 are constrained to be in *even*", known as the set of odd integers.

A point of possible confusion is that a new concept is shown above to be formed when computing an intersection. The propagations are presented in this manner to show how constraints come together to compose new concepts. In the LEX/STABB implementation, a new concept is formed when the operator is applied in the backward direction to compute the preimage, not when the intersection is computed. This is because computations such as $\lfloor c/2 \rfloor$ are performed when computing bindings. The $\lfloor c/2 \rfloor$ is part of the operator language, see section 4.1.7, not the concept description language. Consider op51; the LHS is (^ fr c1), the RHS is (^ (^ fr 2) c2), FORWARD is (c2 . (quotient c2 2)), and BACKWARD is (c1 . {x|match(c2,[x/2])}. In the actual propagation, the intersection of $c2$ and k is k. The new symbol, conveniently called *even* here, is defined as a recognition predicate {x|match('k,[x/2])}. Finally c1 is bound to *even*.

The definition constructed for "even integer" was $\{x|match('k,[x/2])\}$. Because op50 is defined to operate on a real number c, the new concept was assimilated as a specialization of c. The new concept should have been assimilated as a specialization of the integers k. Section 6.5.1 discusses an exact method that would do this.

There was a problem computing the intersection of $\int poly^k(f(x)) \cdot f'(x) \cdot dx$ and the range of op52 $1 - sin^2$ equivalently $(1 - id^2)(sin(x))$. Note that the first expression uses $f(x)$ as well as $f'(x)$. The $f'(x)$ indicates that it is the derivative of $f(x)$. The $f'(x)$ is thus sensitive to the context $f(x)$. The LEX concept description language does not provide this kind of context sensitivity. LEX can represent a similar description $\int poly^k(f(x)) \cdot g(x) \cdot dx$, but is incapable of describing the constraint that the derivative of $f(x)$ be equal to $g(x) \cdot dx$. The intersection algorithm computes trivially that $f \cap sin$ is sin, but notice that f' must then be cos. This problem is a direct result of using the context-free grammar formalism when a context-sensitive formalism is needed. A relational formalism such as Porter's can be used to represent such context sensitivity[44]. Because the formalism contributes bias, mechanisms that shift bias must address choice and change of formalism. The ability to identify exactly those elements of bias that come from a given formalism is an important open research question.

Lenat's AM also creates the concept of even integers, but for completely different reasons. STABB and AM [20] each create the set of even integers by operating on the set of integers, i.e. multiply each element in the set of integers by 2. AM creates such concepts as a part of its discovery process. It generates a new concept, adds it to its knowledge base, and then proceeds with generation of new information based on what is on the agenda of interesting things to do. In contrast, STABB deduces that the concept "even integer" needs to be describable, and then creates the concept in a goal-directed manner to satisfy a specific need.

There are two points to note regarding op50. First, Op50 is not mathematically correct when the value of the function f is negative. Squaring the value of the given function will change a negative value to a positive value, and the principal nth root of a positive real is positive [58]. However, LEX does not have such knowledge regarding such limitations on the laws of exponents. The experiment shows that STABB was able to define a useful concept, "even integer", by deducing a class of problems for which the sequence does work. Application of op50 when the exponent is odd is mathematically illegal when f(x) has a negative value. LEX applies op50 illegally in such cases, and simply cannot progress when, later on in the solution sequence, there is a polynomial raised to a non-integer power. Thus, STABB learned about "even integer" from an operator sequence that reached a conclusion only when an exponent was even. An improvement to LEX would be to have it detect mathematical inconsistency in an operator. For example, if LEX could itself identify the mathematical problem with the law of exponents for a negative base and an even exponent, it would have a second method for learning about even integers as well as a method for detecting mathematical inconsistency in op50.

Second, Op50 had to be added specifically so that the problem could be solved. This is due to the fact that LEX is a forward search problem solver. The entire reason that LEX should rewrite $cos^c(x)$ as $(cos^2(x))^{c/2}$, mathematical correctness notwithstanding, is so that op52 ($cos^2 \rightarrow 1 - sin^2$) can be applied. The actual chain of reasoning used by a human is probably some form of backward reasoning, e.g. means-ends analysis [41]. For example, the reasoning could proceed:

1. To obtain a simple polynomial, work toward using the change of variable operator (op43).

2. To set up the integrand for change of variable, work toward introducing sin.

3. To introduce sin, work toward introducing a cos^2 so that op52 can transform it into $1 - sin^2$.

4. To create a cos^2, use the law of exponents.

LEX cannot do means-ends analysis however, so op50 was necessary.

6.3.2   Experiment #2

For this experiment, the details of the circumstances that led to invocation of the Constraint Back-Propagation procedure are omitted. One step of the solution sequence used op22, which evaluates an indicated multiplication.

$$5 \cdot 6 \tag{6.15}$$

Applying op22, $c_1 \cdot c_2 \rightarrow [c_1 \cdot c_2]$, produces

$$30 \tag{6.16}$$

The constraints that propagated backward through the solution sequence led to the set of real numbers c being back-propagated through op22. Op22 in the backward direction computes the preimage by rewriting the term in the range as the product of two expressions.

$$c_3 \tag{6.17}$$

Intersect the range of op22, $c_1 \cdot c_2 \rightarrow [c_1 \cdot c_2]$, with c_3 producing

$$c_4 \cdot (c_3/c_4)$$

Applying op22 in the backward direction produces

$$c_4 \cdot (c_3/c_4) \tag{6.18}$$

The result of propagating c_3 backward through op22 was $c_4 \cdot (c_3/c_4)$, an expression for the set of all factorizations of c_3. Note that $c_4 \cdot (c_3/c_4)$ is already describable in the description language. Because this set was describable, it was not necessary to construct new descriptions for this propagation step.

Nevertheless, the back-propagation step failed because the deduced set $c_4 \cdot (c_3/c_4)$ did not satisfy a safety check included in the Constraint Back-Propagation procedure. The check requires that a deduced set, in this case $c_4 \cdot (c_3/c_4)$, match the state that occurred in the original solution sequence, in this case $5 \cdot 6$. Although the grammar defines c to be more general than 5, the grammar does not define c/c to be more general than 6. The grammar does not contain rules that allow c/c to grammatically derive 6. 6 is a rational number and is therefore a specific instance of k/k which is a specialization of c/c. The LEX grammar does not have the grammar rules $k/k \rightarrow rational$ and $rational \rightarrow k$ that would permit the match of c_3/c_4 and 6.

Op22 is correct. The safety check simply exposed an inconsistency in the knowledge assumed by the author of op22 and the knowledge actually embedded in LEX's grammar. Such findings present opportunities to acquire additional knowledge. It would be an improvement to LEX if it were made to show the inconsistency to an expert, and ask a question like:

> For this reasoning to be correct, 6 must be a specialization of c_3/c_4. Tell me those new grammar rules that should be added.

6.3.3   Experiment #3

LEX was given the problem $\int x^2 \cdot dx$ which was solved by op2.

$$\int x^2 \cdot dx \qquad (6.19)$$

Applying op2, $\int x^{cnm} \cdot dx \rightarrow x^{[cnm+1]}/[cnm + 1]$, produces

$$(x^3/3) \qquad (6.20)$$

LEX omits the constant of integration c.

The Constraint Back-Propagation procedure was applied to the solution sequence to see whether the procedure would find a constrained domain for op2, even though there had been no need to shift the bias. The idea of using the Constraint Back-Propagation procedure to learn LEX's heuristics more directly is appealing and has yet to be explored thoroughly. The idea is discussed below in section 6.5.5.

Intersecting the range of op2, $\int x^{cnm} \cdot dx \rightarrow x^{[cnm+1]}/[cnm + 1]$, with the set of solved states ax produces

$$x^{cnz}/cnz \qquad (6.21)$$

This is because where $[cnm + 1]$ is shown above, the operator range has cnz. The binding of cnz is to the result of adding 1 to the bound value of cnm. Applying op2 in the backward direction produces

$$\int u^{NS} \cdot du \qquad (6.22)$$

The new concept NS was defined as $\{x|match('cnz,[x+1]\}$ and assimilated as a specialization of cnm. The assimilation procedure was not able to determine that $NS = cnm$. The set NS contains those numbers that are one less than some number in cnz. The set cnz contains all numbers except for 0 so the set NS contains all numbers except for -1. This is exactly the definition of cnm. The result is an unneeded concept in the concept description language. It is well defined and correctly assimilated however so no harm was done.

The inability to notice such set equivalences could lead to trouble however. For example, if a new concept matches cnm to a result and the new concept is assimilated as a specialization of cnz, then a circular definition will exist, leading to infinite recursion. Call-graphs can be used to detect such cycles but were not included in STABB.

6.4   Example Trace

This section shows an annotated trace of the Constraint Back-Propagation procedure for the last two propagation steps of experiment #1. Lines printed by the program are shown in small teletype font.

The operator sequence SEQ1 shows the two positive training instances by operators op51 and op50. The structure of each positive instance includes some information that is not important for the discussion, so that information has been removed. Such omissions are indicated as ''-omitted-''.

```
*(sprint seq1]
((-omitted-
   (INT ((^ COS 7) X))
   (OP51 (INT ((==> (^ FR3 C2)
                    (^ COS 7)
                    ((--> ^ ^)
                    (--> FR3
                         (--> PRIM
                              (--> TRANS
                                   (--> TRIG (--> COS COS)))))
                    (--> C
                         (--> CPRIM
                              (--> CNZ
                                   (--> CNMZ (--> KNMZ 7)))))
               ))
          X))
```

```
                 -omitted-
                 -omitted-
                 -omitted-))
   (-omitted-
    (INT ((* (^ COS 6) COS) X))
    (OP50 (INT ((* (==> (^ FR1 C2)
                        (^ COS 6)
                        ((--> ^ ^)
                         (--> FR1
                              (--> PRIM
                                   (--> TRANS
                                        (--> TRIG (--> COS COS)))))
                        (--> C2
                             (--> CPRIM
                                  (--> CNZ
                                       (--> CNMZ (--> KNMZ 6)))))))
                   COS)
                 X))
        -omitted-
        -omitted-
        -omitted-)))
NIL
```

For each of the instances, the structure following the operator name, OP51 and OP50 respectively, is a map that came from Match showing exactly how the domain description of the operator matched the problem state. Interpreting the first map, (^ FR3 C2), the domain of OP51, mapped to (^ COS 7) that was embedded in the larger expression (INT ((^ COS 7) X)). Grammatical derivation of a single symbol to another single symbol is indicated with a single arrow, e.g. (--> KNMZ 6). Successive derivations are nested, e.g. (--> CNMZ (--> KNMZ 6)). Grammatical derivation of a sentential form of more than one symbol to another sentential form is indicated with a double arrow, e.g.

```
(==> (^ FR1 C2) (^ COS 6)
     ( (--> ^ ^) (--> FR1 (... COS)) (--> C2 (... 6))))
```

Interpreting the second map, (^ FR1 C2), the domain of OP50, mapped to (^ COS 6) that was embedded in the larger expression (INT ((* (^ COS 6) COS) X)).

PAT1 is the set that is assumed to have propagated back from preceding steps.

```
*(sprint pat1]
(INT ((* (^ (^ COS 2) K) COS) AFR))
NIL
```

The Constraint Back-Propagation procedure was called directly.

```
*(back-propagate seq1 pat1]

   Intersecting range of OP50 and pattern
      Range:    (^ (^ FR1 2) C3)
      Pattern:  (INT ((* (^ (^ COS 2) K) COS) AFR))
      Result:   ((INT ((* (^ (^ COS 2) K) COS) AFR)))
```

The procedure defines a new description called N22S that is equivalent to "even". Every expression in the grammar is marked with either PAT or FUN to indicate to the matcher whether the expression is a pattern or a recognition predicate. The function MY*QUO attempts to divide its first argument by its second argument. If a legal numeric division can be performed then the returned value is the result of the division. If a legal numeric division cannot be performed, then the returned value is a symbolic description. For example, (MY*QUO 4 2) returns 2, but (MY*QUO 'SIN 2) returns '(\ SIN 2). The NO-INTO-MAPS flag forces Match to return only "onto" maps (section 4.1.6).

```
   Adding grammar rule to CDL:
     (PAT . N22S)
       ==>
     (FUN LAMBDA (LVAR)
            (MATCH 'K (MY*QUO LVAR 2.0) '(NO-INTO-MAPS)))
```

The Constraint Back-Propagation procedure assimilates N22S as a specialization of "C", i.e. any numeric expression. This is discussed below.

```
   Adding grammar rule to CDL:
     (PAT . C) ==> (PAT . N22S)
```

The result of the back propagation step is a set of states for which the operator sequence works in the forward direction for $\int cos^{N22S}(x) \cdot cos(x) \cdot dx$.

```
Back-propagation via backward OP50
  Result:    (((INT ((* (^ COS N22S) COS) AFR))
              ((^ . ^) (^ . ^) (FR1 . COS) (2 . 2)
                  (C3 . K) (C2 . N22S))))

Intersecting range of OP51 and pattern
  Range:     (* (^ FR1 C1) FR2)
  Pattern:   (INT ((* (^ COS N22S) COS) AFR))
  Result:    ((INT ((* (^ COS N22S) COS) AFR)))
```

The procedure defines a new description called N24S that is equivalent to "odd". Note that the recognition predicate for N24S calls the recognition predicate for N22S. The function RADD1 attempts to add 1 to its argument. If the addition can be performed then the returned value is the result of the addition. If the addition cannot be performed, then the returned value is a symbolic description. For example, (RADD1 2) returns 3, but (RADD1 'SIN) returns '(+ 1 SIN).

```
Adding grammar rule to CDL:
  (PAT . N24S)
   ==>
  (FUN LAMBDA (LVAR) (MATCH 'N22S (RADD1 LVAR) '(NO-INTO-MAPS)))
```

The procedure assimilates N24S as a specialization of "C", i.e. any numeric expression.

```
Adding grammar rule to CDL:
  (PAT . C) ==> (PAT . N24S)
```

The result of the back propagation step is a set of states for which the operator sequence works in the forward direction for $\int cos^{N24S}(x) \cdot dx$.

```
Back-propagation via backward OP51
  Result:    (((INT ((^ COS N24S) AFR))
             ((* . *)
              (^ . ^)
              (FR1 . COS)
              (C1 . N22S)
              (FR2 . COS)
              (C2 . N24S)
              (FR3 . COS))))
```

```
((INT ((^ COS N24S) AFR))
   ((* . *) (^ . ^) (FR1 . COS) (C1 . N22S) (FR2 . COS)
   (C2 . N24S) (FR3 . COS))))
```

6.5 Discussion

Six issues became apparent from the experiments. First, assimilation of concept descriptions represented as predicates is a nontrivial problem. Second, it is difficult to detect synonymous descriptions that are represented as recognition predicates. Third, a formalism in which a description language is expressed can itself introduce bias. Fourth, there is interaction between the operator language and concept description language that requires consideration by a program author. Fifth, deducing constrained domains of applicability for an operator leads to the possibility of computing a strong and correct bias without observing training instances. Sixth, applying Constraint Back-Propagation to subgoals may be fruitful.

6.5.1 Knowledge Based Assimilation

This section discusses a knowledge-based procedure for assimilating new descriptions that are represented as recognition predicates. The approach could lead to better assimilation than the approach that was implemented in the Constraint Back-Propagation procedure of STABB.

Assimilation of the description for even integer could have been done correctly in the first experiment in the following way. An alternative definition of even integer is $\{y | (\exists x \in k | y = 2 \cdot x)\}$. This definition can be generated mechanically as easily as that currently generated by STABB. From the Constraint Back-Propagation, it is known that x and 2 are integers. If it were also known that the integers are closed under multiplication, then a procedure could easily prove that every y is also an integer. The critical piece of knowledge for the proof is that the integers are closed under multiplication.

How could a learning program construct such a proof? First, the program needs to know what to try to prove. It is known that the new concept is the set of elements in which each is equivalent to 2 times some integer. It is also known that the set under which to assimilate the new term is no more general than the set of real numbers. [2] The program could exhaustively

---

[2]Note that although the description language does not contain the explicit axiom that

consider those generalizations of $[2 \cdot k]$ in the existing concept description language that are more specific or equal to the set of numbers c. In LEX's description language, some of those generalizations are $[k \cdot k]$, $[2 \cdot r]$, $[k \cdot r]$, and $[r \cdot r]$. The number of possible generalizations of $[2 \cdot k]$ in the LEX description language that are not more general than c is 29, i.e. small. There are 3 terms more general than or equal to k, and 10 terms more general than or equal to 2, giving 30-1=29 proper generalizations. If the program does not have any knowledge about these sets, it could query an expert. It would be a pleasant surprise for a learning program to ask such intelligent questions as "Are the integers closed under multiplication?" or in mechanical terms "Is the result of $[k \cdot k]$ always k?". The key idea is that a program might find something useful about $[2 \cdot k]$ by trying to find out something about more general forms, such as $[k \cdot k]$.

When the expert provides additional knowledge, the learning program could save the piece of knowledge for potential application in the future. How would the program save such domain knowledge? One simple way is to embed it in the concept description language. For example, one could insert the set $k \cdot k$ as a specialization of k. This would be completely acceptable in LEX's current language and Match function.

The main idea in the above reasoning process is that one starts with a generated definition for a recognition predicate, and then attempts to generalize the statement of the definition to guide the search for an axiom that pertains to the more general expression. Generalization of the statement of the definition is done by generalizing the concept descriptions that appear in the statement of the definition. As soon as a generalized expression is found for which there is an associated axiom, e.g. integers are closed under multiplication, then a concept description has been identified that is a generalization of the synthesized term. This approach identifies knowledge worth having, an important problem for knowledge acquisition programs.

$[c \cdot c]$ always evaluates to a real result, the operator for evaluating multiplications does. It would be a significant improvement for a program such as LEX to be able to use such knowledge already encoded in the operators.

6.5.2   Knowledge Based Set Equivalence

In the third experiment, the Constraint Back-Propagation procedure generated a recognition predicate of the form $\{x|match('cnz, [x + 1])\}$. The procedure assimilated this set as a specialization of cnm even though it was equivalent to cnm. The procedure was not able to determine that the sets were equivalent. This kind of error could lead to infinite recursion if cyclic definitions are inadvertently created. For example, if a new concept is later defined using cnm in the recognition predicate and the concept is assimilated as a specialization of cnz then cnz and cnm each use the other.

Proving set equivalence is difficult in general. A method that looks at set differences may be of use. For example, $cnz - cnm$ is -1 and $cnm - cnz$ is 0. By noting that the -1 is mapped to 0 via the $+1$ operation in the recognition predicate and by knowing that for any element $z \in cnz, \exists y \in cnm|y = z+1$ it can be concluded that the set $cnz+1$ is equal to the set cnm. This knowledge is already expressed in op2 because it maps any value in the domain of cnm via $+1$ to a value in the range cnz.

Synonymous descriptions in the language is not harmful by itself. A problem arises when circular definitions are created. It may be easier to detect and remove cyclic definitions by the use of a call-graph than it is to prove set equivalence.

6.5.3   Bias in Formalism of Description Language

As shown in section 6.3.1, the intersection algorithm was inadequate because it could not handle certain context sensitive constraints. In the first experiment there was a need to intersect the description $sin(x)$ with a description that included $f(x)$ *and* $g(x)$, where $g(x)$ was constrained to be the derivative of $f(x)$. The intersection of $sin(x)$ and $f(x)$ was computed easily as $sin(x)$ but, as a result of the inability to specify the derivative constraint for the $g(x)$, there was no knowledge in the intersection algorithm that the $g(x)$ depends on the $f(x)$. To finish the computation, the intersection algorithm would have had to calculate $g(x)$ by computing the derivative of $sin(x)$ as $cos(x)$.

The correspondence between $f(x)$ and $g(x)$ could not be practically represented in LEX's grammar. Thus, intersection failed because it would have had to use the correspondence for its calculation. The LEX formalism is biased against such descriptions. If a biased formalism is employed then an algorithm that shifts bias should be able to shift the formalism as well. More work is needed on understanding the bias of formalisms.

6.5.4   Interaction of Operator Language and Description Language

The grammar for LEX's concept description language uses string rewrite rules. The operators use string rewrites *and* arithmetic rewrites. Thus, through composition of symbolic and arithmetic transformations, it is possible to construct descriptions that are not found in the LEX grammar. This is the reason that Constraint Back-Propagation can be used to deduce new descriptions. The problem solving experience shows which operator sequences should be followed. Back propagation of constraints over such a sequence can yield useful compositions of symbolic and arithmetic transformations. The bias shifting procedure translates any concepts that are defined through an arithmetic composition into recognition predicates that are added to the concept description language.

The operator language and the concept description language were written for different purposes. The experimentation has shown an area in which they interact. Grammar rewrite rules *and* operator rewrite rules each define how one description can be transformed into another. It remains unclear whether such a dichotomy between operator rules and grammar rules is useful or necessary.

In addition to the problem of mixing the two classes of rewrite rules for Constraint Back-Propagation, separate operator language and description language allows unplanned inconsistencies. For example, because the interaction of the operator language and the concept description language was not well understood when each was created, certain liberties were taken when writing the operators. For example, the change of variable operator is

$$\int g(f(x)) \cdot f'(x)dx \rightarrow \int g(u)du$$

One may wonder how the domain of an operator can describe $g(f(x)) \cdot f'(x)$ when the concept description language cannot describe such context-sensitivity. This is possible only because the domain of the operator is described as $\int g(f(x)) \cdot h(x) \cdot dx$, and the code in the operator explicitly tests whether $derivative(f(x)) = h(x)$. If the relation holds, the operator performs the change of variable. If the relation does not hold, the operator rewrites the problem state to include the symbol $fail$, which is not in LEX's grammar. At this point, the problem solver will never be able to proceed to a solution along that branch of the search tree because $fail$ does not appear in the domain of any operator. Several other operators use this $fail$ convention. This is counterproductive however, because LEX then futilely tries to learn a heuristic without the ability to describe the domain of the heuristic in the description language. It is a bad idea to permit descriptive capability in the operator language that is not available in the concept description language.

6.5.5 A Method for Computing a Strong and Correct Bias

Under certain assumptions, it ought to be possible that, for a given **n**, it is possible to compute an initial bias that is strong and correct for problems that can be solved within **n** steps. That is, computation of an initial bias is done prior to observation of any training instances.

Given a set of forward and corresponding backward operators, a description language, and the ability to do Constraint Back-Propagation through any operator, it is possible to deduce the domain of every operator sequence of length $n \geq 1$ that leads to a solution. Descriptions other than those created during Constraint Back-Propagation are unnecessary because only domains of operator sequences ever need to be describable. Consider $n = 0$. The set of states that is solved in 0 steps is the set of solved states. Consider $n = 1$. By intersecting the range of an operator with the set of solved states, application of the backward operator yields the set of states that can be solved with exactly $n = 1$ operator application. Any new descriptions needed for the constraint propagation step are added to the language during the propagation step. Consider $n > 1$. The Constraint Back-Propagation procedure can be used to deduce the domains of the operators that would lead to a state that is solvable in $n - 1$ steps. Thus, it is possible to deduce the domains of all operator sequences of length less than or equal to **n** that lead to a solution.

The major benefit of this approach is that the description language will become sufficiently enriched, such that the domain of a heuristic will be describable in the language (for any operator application involved in a solution sequence of not more than n steps). A drawback of the approach is that only good operator sequences will justify heuristics, so many of the deduced descriptions will never be needed for a heuristic. Nevertheless, the approach does not introduce descriptions that are not needed for describing the domain of *some* operator sequence. In practical applications, one can expect the length of the longest operator sequence to be sufficiently small, e.g. less than 20, making the approach computationally acceptable. For LEX, the longest operator sequence observed is approximately 15 steps. Although there are potentially $|set of operators|^n$ sequences of length n, there will be significant pruning whenever the domain of one operator does not intersect the range of another. Research on finding an initial bias that is strong and correct is an important unexplored area. The author knows of no other work to date on the problem.

This technique can compute a bias that is too weak or, equivalently, a description language that is too rich. There are two reasons.

1. As mentioned above, the language will be able to describe concepts needed for operator sequences that a program like LEX would learn through experience not to use.

2. Useful operator sequences may have the same beginning subsequence and yet diverge at some point. As shown in figure 6.2, if two sequences diverge, then there is no need to distinguish between the two trajectories while still sharing a common path. For example, there is no need to individually describe both the domain of operator sequence $OpA - OpB$ *and* the domain of operator sequence $OpA - OpC$. It is sufficient to be able to describe the domain of operator sequence $OpA - (OpB \lor OpC)$.

Despite computing a bias that is weaker than necessary for describing the heuristics that LEX will ultimately learn, the approach is promising because it computes only domains of applicability that LEX can ever consider, given some set of operators. LEX has no need to describe any other set.

6.5.6   Regressing Sub-Goals

Constraint Back-Propagation is a familiar process but is not always recognized as such. Banerji [3, sec 4.4] presents a form of Constraint Back-

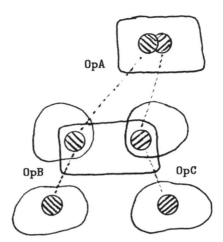

Figure 6.2: Diverging Operator Sequences

Propagation for ticktacktoe. There he shows deduction of the concept "fork".

Consider an informal example from the domain of chess. Note that the set of goal states for the propagation is the set of states in which a gain in the piece advantage is achieved. Improving the piece advantage is an important subgoal in the game of chess because a player who is ahead can trade evenly to increase the significance of his piece advantage. One can deduce sets of states that lead to an increase in the piece advantage. Black's pieces are shown in bold face, white's in plain face. An arrow from x to y indicates that x threatens y. It is white's move.

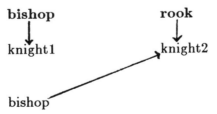

In move #1, White elects to guard his unprotected knight1 with his bishop.

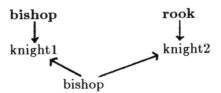

In move #2, Black's bishop captures white's knight1.

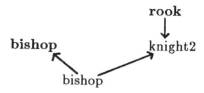

In move #3, White's bishop captures black's bishop.

White has removed his guard for his knight. Black's rook can now safely capture White's knight. White wants to understand what lead to a free capture for his opponent, to ensure that he can avoid giving away a free capture in future play.

Consider a reasoning process based on Constraint Back-Propagation. Assume that White has the conjunctive concept of a "free capture":

```
free.capture(x,y,p1,p2)
  [  it is x's turn
     x has a piece at p1
     x's piece at p1 can move to p2
     y has a piece at p2
     y does not have a piece that can move to p2
  ]
```

White reasons backward through move #3 to see that when he made the capture, the piece he moved had been guarding another White piece. The concept of a "free capture that gives away a free capture" or, with a shorter name, "indirect trade" is deduced:

```
indirect.trade(x,y,p1,p2,p3,p4)
  [  free.capture(x,y,p1,p2)
     y has a piece at p3
     x has a piece at p4
     y's piece at p3 can move to p4
```

```
    x's piece at p1 can move to p4
    if x's piece at p1 were at p2,
        then it could not then move to p4
]
```

White reasons backward through move #2 to see that when black made his capture, black produced a position that was an indirect.trade. The concept of a "capture that leaves an indirect trade" is deduced:

```
capture.leaving.an.indirect.trade(x,y,p1,p2,p3,p4,p5)
    [   it is x's turn
        x has a piece at p3
        x's piece at p3 can move to p4
        y has a piece at p4
        y has a piece at p1
        y's piece at p1 can move to p4
        y has a piece at p5
        y's piece at p1 can move to p5
        if y's piece at p1 were at p5,
            then it could not then move to p4
        x has a piece at p2
        x's piece at p2 can move to p5
    ]
```

White reasons backward through move #1 to see that removing Black's free capture by guarding a threatened piece with a guard that is already guarding some other piece will lead to a capture.leaving.an.indirect.trade for Black.

A player that deduces these concepts and tests possible successor board positions with respect to these concepts, becomes a better chess player. One endeavors to be able to predict consequences of moves based on recognition of patterns, instead of generating and evaluating successor board positions. The main lesson from this example is that Constraint Back-Propagation can serve as a fundamental mechanism for deducing useful classes worth being able to describe.

Chapter 7

Conclusion

This chapter provides a summary of the research, a statement of the results, a discussion of the issues, and an assessment for further work.

7.1 Summary

The role of bias in learning concepts from examples was identified. Bias is the set of influences that collectively cause a learner to favor one hypothesis over another. Because bias accounts for the inductive leaps made by the learner, given the observed instances, it is important to study how the process of learning a good inductive bias can be mechanized.

Representation of bias was discussed. Two broad categories are the procedural and the declarative. Declarative forms were given greater attention because declarative knowledge is more easily manipulated than procedural knowledge.

It was observed that finding a good bias is necessary for good performance on inductive learning tasks. It was noted that much of he effort currently spent in getting good performance from a learning program is devoted to finding a suitable bias. This led to the thesis:

1. Search for a better bias is a fundamental part of the learning task.

2. Search for a better bias can be mechanized.

A parallel between appropriate bias and appropriate representation was drawn. This opened the possibility of learning a good inductive bias by learning a good representation.

Exemplary earlier work was reviewed. Learning programs by Vere, Mitchell, and Michalski were observed to use a static bias. Programs by Waterman and Lenat employ a dynamic bias.

The RTA Method was put forth as one way of mechanizing the search for a better bias. Five simplifications were adopted:

1. Focus on the problem of shifting from one bias to another. Ignore the problem of determining an original bias.

2. Represent bias as a restricted hypothesis space, defined by an incomplete concept description language.

3. Consider the problem of shifting bias within a formalism. Do not consider the problems of shifting formalism or identifying characteristic bias associated with any particular formalism.

4. Consider the problem of weakening a strong bias by adding new descriptions to the concept description language. Do not consider the problem of strengthening a weak bias by eliminating descriptions from the concept description language.

5. Shift bias when the space of hypotheses being searched by the concept learner does not include a concept that is consistent with the observed training instances.

The method was used in the STABB program which was added to the LEX learning program. When LEX cannot find any consistent concept description, it invokes STABB to shift LEX's bias so that LEX will be able to find at least one consistent description. STABB gives LEX the ability to learn inductive bias.

Two algorithms were designed and incorporated in STABB, each using the RTA Method. The first was Least Disjunction, which constructs new concept descriptions for the concept description language that would otherwise need to be described via disjunction. The second was Constraint Back-Propagation, which constructs new concept descriptions that are consistent with the observed instances and describe domains of useful operator sequences.

Finally, experiments were performed so that the behavior of LEX and STABB could be observed.

7.2   Results

The main result is the demonstration of the thesis. It is indeed possible for a mechanical procedure to learn inductive bias. This research reports one way of learning inductive bias; more work is needed before any theory of shifting bias can be attempted.

A second result is the RTA Method for shifting bias. The method makes explicit the three steps of recommending new descriptions, translating the recommendations into new descriptions, and assimilating the new descriptions in the concept description language.

Additional results are the Least Disjunction procedure, the Constraint Back-Propagation procedure, and identification of issues.

7.3   Issues

A number of issues emerged both from the design of STABB and from pondering its performance.

7.3.1   Role of Bias

The role of bias is an issue for anyone building an inductive learning program. Given a set of observed instances, the space of all possible consistent hypotheses contains both good and bad hypotheses. Bias accounts for the choices made. A good choice of hypothesis results in effective learning while choice of a bad hypothesis results in failure. Finding a good bias is part of the learning problem.

7.3.2   Sources of Bias

The sources of bias need to be identified and understood. The learning algorithm can encode bias procedurally. The concept description language and the language formalism can encode bias declaratively. Bias can be encoded explicitly as preference criteria to be followed by the learning algorithm.

7.3.3   When to Shift

It is necessary to define a criterion for when to shift bias. The criterion used for STABB is to shift when LEX cannot find any concept description consistent with the observed instances. Other criteria may be appropriate, such as poor performance during classification or being told that no further training instances will be presented.

7.3.4   Strength of Bias

A fundamental concern is whether to strengthen or weaken bias. STABB weakens bias by adding new concept descriptions to the concept description language. An alternate approach is to strengthen bias by identifying and removing descriptions from the concept description language. The ability to strengthen bias would be useful for the Least Disjunction procedure because descriptions that it has added can later become obsolete.

7.3.5   How to Shift Bias

A set of issues relates to how bias is manipulated by a learning program. This depends on many factors, such as the representation (source) of the bias, the learning algorithm, the criteria for when to shift, and the overall strategy for weakening the bias. The remaining issues follow from adopting the RTA Method and its assumptions.

7.3.6   Recommending New Descriptions

Recommending new concept descriptions is heuristically driven because the concept to be learned is not known prior to learning. Deciding which new descriptions to make available to the concept learner is a critical step in building a program that learns inductive bias. For Least Disjunction, the heuristic was:

> *If a new consistent description is needed, then construct a new description that is a least specific disjunction of existing descriptions.*

For Constraint Back-Propagation, the heuristic was:

> *If an operator sequence leads to a solution then create a new concept description that describes the domain of the operator sequence.*

7.3.7   Translating Recommendations

Translating recommendations into new descriptions in the formalism of the concept description language is important not only for the process of adding new descriptions to the concept description language but also for efficiency. For example, a heuristic of the form:

Apply op50 if it leads to a solution.

describes the heuristic for op50 in a correct yet useless manner. A heuristic is useful only if overall search effort is reduced. The translation step for Least Disjunction is to alter the concept description language so that needed disjunctions are implicit in the definitions, not explicit in the descriptions. The translation step for Constraint Back-Propagation is to evaluate the recommendation, thereby changing function calls such as *intersection*() and *preimage* to descriptions.

7.3.8   Assimilating New Descriptions

Assimilating new descriptions depends on the representation of the hypothesis space and the organization of the hypotheses. For LEX, a new description can be assimilated by adding grammar rules that link old descriptions to the new. A more difficult problem than the mechanics of adding a new description is the problem of determining those descriptions in the concept description language that are immediately more general. For Least Disjunction assimilation was straight-forward. For Constraint Back-Propagation the problem was complicated by the fact that new descriptions are defined as recognition predicates. Determining the correct placement of the new description can require proof of subset or set equivalence relationships, a difficult problem when the descriptions are functional rather than structural.

7.3.9   Side Effects

A problem that arises from changing the bias is that assumptions based on the previous bias may no longer hold. For example, the version space boundary sets define the space of all consistent hypotheses in the concept description language. When a new (revised) concept description language is substituted, the version space may no longer contain all the consistent hypotheses. There is a general problem of how to re-establish correct assumptions. The issue was avoided for STABB and LEX by recomputing the version space. That requires reprocessing the training instances which is undesirable. When many version spaces exist, based on a single concept description language, the problem is magnified.

7.3.10   Multiple Uses of Concept Description Language

Inconsistencies can arise when using the concept description language for multiple purposes. For example, LEX uses the concept description language both for describing heuristics and for describing domains and ranges of the operators. In experiment #2 with Constraint Back-Propagation, $c_1 \div c_2$ needed to match 12 because of the way in which the backward operator was defined. This was not the case however because the LEX concept description language does not contain the concept of a rational number $k_1 \div k_2$ of 12 is an instance. Reconciliation of grammar rules and operator rules must be considered.

7.4   Further Work

The issues presented above are all candidates for further consideration. In addition, two research directions emerged that show promise.

First, to be able to complete an assimilation task, the learner may need knowledge that it does not currently possess. By examining generalized forms of the new description, the learner is guided toward the needed knowledge that it lacks. For example, to determine whether the set of even integers is a subset of the set of integers, it would be sufficient to know that the integers are closed under multiplication by 2. Acquiring this rule or the more general rule that the integers are closed under multiplication becomes a useful knowledge acquisition problem.

Second, the Constraint Back-Propagation procedure augments Waldinger's goal-regression by providing the ability to construct efficient new descriptions. Further exploration of this kind of deductive learning is in order. One avenue is to explore whether Constraint Back-Propagation can be used to enrich the concept description language before any problems are solved. Further, by then considering operator application costs it might be possible to use dynamic programming to speed the learning task. A second avenue, as proposed in section 6.5.6, is to explore the use of Constraint Back-Propagation on subgoals. Improvement at solving subgoals leads to improved solving of supergoals.

Bibliography

[1] Amarel, S., "On Representations of Problems of Reasoning about Actions", *Machine Intelligence*, University of Edinburgh Press, Vol. 3, 1968.

[2] Banerji, R. B., "Pattern Recognition: Structural Description Languages", *Encyclopedia of Computer Science and Technology*, Belzer, Holzman and Kent (Eds.), Marcel Dekker, New York, 1979, pp. 1.

[3] Banerji, R. B., *Artificial Intelligence: a Theoretical Approach*, Elsevier North Holland, New York, 1980.

[4] Bruner, J. S., Goodnow, J. J. and Austin, G. A., *A Study of Thinking*, Wiley, New York, 1956.

[5] Buchanan, B. G. and Mitchell, T. M., "Model-Directed Learning of Production Rules", *Pattern-Directed Inference Systems*, Waterman, D. A. and Hayes-Roth, F. (Eds.), Academic Press, New York, 1978.

[6] Carbonell, J. G., "Towards a Self-Extending Parser", *Proceedings of the 17th Meeting of the Association for Computational Linguistics*, 1979, pp. 3-7.

[7] Dieterich, T. G. and Michalski, R. S., "Learning and generalization of characteristic descriptions: evaluation criteria and comparative review of selected methods", *Sixth International Joint Conference on Artificial Intelligence*, Tokyo, Japan, August 1979, pp. 223-231.

[8] Ernst, G. and Newell, A., *GPS: A Case Study in Generality and Problem Solving*, Academic Press, Inc., New York, ACM Monograph, 1969.

[9] Fikes, R. E. and Nilsson, N. J., "STRIPS: A New Approach to the Application of Theorem Proving to Problem Solving", *Artificial Intelligence*, Vol. 2, 1971, pp. 189-208.

[10] Fikes, R. E., Hart, P. E. and Nilsson, N. J., "Learning and Executing Generalized Robot Plans", *Artificial Intelligence*, Vol. 3, 1972, pp. 251-288.

[11] Guralnik, D. B. (Ed.), *Webster's New World Dictionary of the American Language*, The World Publishing Company, New York and Cleveland, 1970.

[12] Hayes-Roth, F. and McDermott, J., "An Interference Matching Technique for Inducing Abstractions", *Communications of the ACM*, Vol. 21, No. 5, 1978, pp. 401-410.

[13] Hopcroft, J. E. and Ullman, J. D., *Formal Languages and their Relation to Automata*, Addison-Wesley, Reading, Mass., 1969.

[14] Hunt, E. B. and Hovland, C. I., "Programming a model of human concept formation", *Computers and Thought*, Feigenbaum, E. A. and Feldman, J. (Eds.), McGraw-Hill, New York, 1963, pp. 310-325.

[15] Iba, G. A., "Learning disjunctive concepts from examples", Master's thesis, M.I.T., 1979, (also AI memo 548).

[16] Keller, R. M., "Learning by Re-Expressing Concepts for Efficient Recognition", *Proceedings of the National Conference on Artificial Intelligence*, American Association for Artificial Intelligence, August 1983, pp. 182-186.

[17] Kelly, V. E. and Steinberg, L. I., "The Critter System: Analyzing Digital Circuits by Propagating Behaviors and Specifications", *Proceedings of the National Conference on Artificial Intelligence*, American Association for Artificial Intelligence, August 1982, pp. 284-289.

[18] Koffman, E. B., "Learning Through Pattern Recognition Applied to a Class of Games", *IEEE Transactions on Systems Science and Cybernetics*, Vol. SSC-4, No. 1, March 1968, pp. 12-16.

[19] Langley, P. W., *Descriptive Discovery Processes: Experiments in Baconian Science*, Ph.D. dissertation, Carnegie-Mellon, May 1980.

[20] Lenat, D. B., *AM: An Artificial Intelligence Approach to Discovery in Mathematics as Heuristic Search*, Ph.D. dissertation, Stanford University, 1976.

[21] Lenat, D. B., "The Role of Heuristics in Learning by Discovery: Three Case Studies", *Machine Learning*, Michalski, R. S., Carbonell, J. G. and Mitchell, T. M. (Eds.), Tioga, Palo Alto, 1982.

[22] Lenat, D. B., "The Nature of Heuristics II: Background and Examples", *Artificial Intelligence*, North Holland, Vol. 21, No. 1/2, March 1983, pp. 31-59.

[23] Meltzer, B., "The Semantics of Induction and the Possibility of Complete Systems of Inductive Inference", *Artificial Intelligence*, Vol. 1, 1970, pp. 189-192.

[24] Michalski, R. S., "Pattern recognition as rule-guided inductive inference", *IEEE Transactions on Pattern Analysis and Machine Intelligence*, Vol. PAMI-2, No. 4, 1980, pp. 349-361.

[25] Michalski, R. S. and Chilausky, R. L., "Learning by being told and learning from examples: an experimental comparison of the two methods of knowledge acquisition in the context of developing an expert system for soybean disease diagnosis", *Policy Analysis and Information Systems*, Vol. 4, No. 2, June 1980, (Special issue on knowledge acquisition and induction).

[26] Michalski, R. S., Carbonell, R. S. and Mitchell, T. M. (Eds.), *Machine Learning*, Tioga, Palo Alto, C.A., 1983.

[27] Michalski, R. S., "A Theory and Methodology of Inductive Learning", *Machine Learning*, Michalski, R. S., Carbonell, J. G. and Mitchell, T. M. (Eds.), Tioga, Palo Alto, 1983.

[28] Michalski, R. S. and Stepp, R., "Learning from Observation: Conceptual Clustering", *Machine Learning*, Michalski, R. S., Carbonell, J. G. and Mitchell, T. M. (Eds.), Tioga, Palo Alto, 1983.

[29] Michalski, R. S., "A Theory and Methodology of Inductive Learning", *Artificial Intelligence*, North Holland, Vol. 20, No. 2, February 1983, pp. 111-161.

[30] Minton, S., "Constraint-based Generalization: Learning Game-Playing Plans from Single Examples", *Proceedings of the National Conference on Artificial Intelligence*, 1984, pp. 251-254.

[31] Mitchell, T. M., "Version Spaces: A candidate elimination approach to rule learning", *Fifth International Joint Conference on Artificial Intelligence*, Cambridge, Mass., 1977, pp. 305-310.

[32] Mitchell, T. M., *Version Spaces: An approach to concept learning*, Ph.D. dissertation, Stanford University, December 1978, (also Stanford CS report STAN-CS-78-711, HPP-79-2).

[33] Mitchell, T. M., "The need for biases in learning generalizations", Technical Report CBM-TR-117, Department of Computer Science, Rutgers University, May 1980.

[34] Mitchell, T. M., Utgoff, P. E., Nudel, B. and Banerji, R., "Learning problem-solving heuristics through practice", *Proceedings of the Seventh International Joint Conference on Artificial Intelligence*, Vancouver, August 1981, pp. 127-134.

[35] Mitchell, T. M., "Generalization as Search", *Artificial Intelligence*, Vol. 18, No. 2, March 1982, pp. 203-226.

[36] Mitchell, T. M., Utgoff, P. E. and Banerji, R. B., "Learning by Experimentation: Acquiring and Refining Problem-Solving Heuristics", *Machine Learning*, Michalski, R. S., Carbonell, J. G. and Mitchell, T. M. (Eds.), Tioga, 1983.

[37] Mitchell, T. M., "Toward Combining Empirical and Analytic Methods for Learning Heuristics", *Human and Artificial Intelligence*, Elithorn, A. and Banerji, R. (Eds.), Erlbaum, 1983.

[38] Mostow, D. J., *Mechanical Transformation of Task Heuristics into Operational Procedures*, Ph.D. dissertation, Carnegie-Mellon University, 1981.

[39] Mostow, D. J., "Machine Transformation of Advice into a Heuristic Search Procedure", *Machine Learning*, Michalski, R. S., Carbonell, J. G. and Mitchell, T. M. (Eds.), Tioga Press, Palo Alto, 1983.

[40] Munkres, J. R., *Topology A First Course*, Prentice-Hall, 1975.

[41] Newell, A. and Simon, H., *Human Problem Solving*, Prentice-Hall, Englewood Cliffs, N.J., 1982.

[42] Nilsson, N. J., *Problem-Solving Methods in Artificial Intelligence*, MacGraw-Hill, 1971.

[43] Politakis, P. G., *Using Empirical Analysis to Refine Expert System Knowledge Bases*, Ph.D. dissertation, Rutgers University, October 1982, (also Tech. Report CBM-TR-130).

[44] Porter, B., "Learning Problem Solving", Ph.D. Dissertation, Computer Science Department, Uuniversity of California at Irvine, 1984.

[45] Royden, H. L., *Real Analysis*, Macmillan, New York, 1968.

[46] Sammut, C., *Learning Concepts by Performing Experiments*, Ph.D. dissertation, University of New South Wales, November 1981.

[47] Samuel, A. L., "Some Studies in Machine Learning using the Game of Checkers", *Computers and Thought*, Feigenbaum, E. A. and Feldman, J. (Eds.), McGraw-Hill, New York, 1963, pp. 71-105.

[48] Samuel, A. L., "Some Studies in Machine Learning using the Game of Checkers II - Recent Progress", *IBM Journal of Research and Development*, Vol. 11, No. 6, 1967, pp. 601-617.

[49] Shapiro, Ehud Y., "Inductive Inference of Theories From Facts", Research Report 192, Yale University, February 1981.

[50] Smith, R. G., Mitchell, T. M., Chestek, R. A. and Buchanan, B. G., "A Model for Learning Systems", *Fifth International Joint Conference on Artificial Intelligence*, Cambridge, Mass., 1977, pp. 338-343.

[51] Stallman, R. M. and Sussman, G. J., "Forward Reasoning and Dependency-Directed Backtracking in a System for Computer-Aided Circuit Analysis", *Artificial Intelligence*, North Holland, Vol. 9, 1977, pp. 135-196.

[52] Stefik, M. J., *Planning with Constraints*, Ph.D. dissertation, Stanford University, January 1980, (Computer Science Department Report STAN-CS-80-784).

[53] Swokowski, E. W., *Calculus with Analytic Geometry*, Prindle, Weber & Schmidt, Incorporated, Boston, 1975.

[54] Utgoff, P. E., "Acquisition of Appropriate Bias for Inductive Concept Learning", Thesis Proposal, Department of Computer Science, Rutgers University, May 1982.

[55] Utgoff, P. E., "Adjusting Bias in Concept Learning", *Proceedings of the International Workshop on Machine Learning*, Monticello, Illinois, May 1983, pp. 105-109, (shorter version in *Proceedings of the Eighth International Joint Conference on Artificial Intelligence*, Karlsruhe, August 1983, pp. 447-449).

[56] Utgoff, P. E., *Shift of Bias for Inductive Concept Learning*, Ph.D. dissertation, Rutgers University, October 1984.

[57] Utgoff, P. E. and Mitchell, T. M., "Acquisition of Appropriate Bias for Inductive Concept Learning", *Proceedings of the National Conference on Artificial Intelligence*, American Association for Artificial Intelligence, August 1982, pp. 414-417.

[58] Vance, E. P., *An Introduction to Modern Mathematics*, Addison-Wesley, Reading, Mass., 1968, (second edition).

[59] Vere, S. A., "Induction of Relational Productions in the Presence of Background Information", *Proceedings of the Fifth International Joint Conference on Artificial Intelligence*, Cambridge, Mass., 1977, pp. 349-355.

[60] Vere, S. A., "Multilevel counterfactuals for generalizations of relational concepts and productions", *Artificial Intelligence*, Vol. 14, No. 2, September 1980, pp. 138-164.

[61] Waldinger, R., "Achieving Several Goals Simultaneously", *Machine Intelligence*, Elcock, E. W. and Michie, D. (Eds.), John Wiley & Sons Inc., New York, 1976, pp. 94-136.

[62] Waterman, D. A., "Generalization learning techniques for automating the learning of heuristics", *Artificial Intelligence*, Vol. 1, No. 1/2, 1970, pp. 121-170.

[63] Winston, P. H., "Learning Structural Descriptions from Examples", *The Psychology of Computer Vision*, Winston, P. H. (Ed.), McGraw Hill, New York, 1975, ch. 5.

Appendix A

Lisp Code

Below is code for STABB and related portions of LEX. All of the STABB code and most of the LEX code that is included here was written by the author. Other contributors to LEX have been Tom Mitchell, Rich Keller, Bill Bogdan, Bernard Nudel, and Adam Irgon.

The LEX Generalizer (not included) was modified both to save the training instances and to call STABB when a version space would otherwise become empty.

The top-level function of STABB is REVISE-CDL. The functions called by REVISE-CDL and the major data structures are grouped into sections below. Entries within each section are listed in alphabetical order.

A.1   STABB

These functions comprise STABB. The top-level function is REVISE-CDL, called by the LEX Generalizer.

```
(DE ADDITIONAL-BINDINGS (BINDING PATTERN)
  {;; Make up a binding for any atom in PATTERN which is
     not bound in BINDING.}
  (AND PATTERN
    (COND
      [(ATOM PATTERN)
       (COND
         [(ASSOC PATTERN BINDING) NIL]
         [T (NCONS (CONS PATTERN PATTERN))])]
      [T (MAPCONC
           (F:L (PAT*) (ADDITIONAL-BINDINGS BINDING PAT*))
```

104

```
          PATTERN)])))

(DE ASSIMILATE-DISJUNCTION (POS-HDESCRS NEG-HDESCRS HNAME)
  {;; POS-HDESCRS is the least disjunction. Want
      to compute and make most general changes to language
      such that disjunction becomes describable without making
      such description(s) also cover any negative.}
  {;; Returns T if language revised, else NIL}
  (AND \DEBUG-LEAST-DISJUNCTION
    (MSG O "Least-disjunction hdescrs are:"
      (E (MAPC (F:L (H) (PRINHDESCR H 3)) POS-HDESCRS))
      O "Negative instances hdescrs are:"
      (E (MAPC (F:L (H) (PRINHDESCR H 3)) NEG-HDESCRS))))
  (WITH [(MGDS
           (MOST-GENERAL-DISJUNCTIONS
             POS-HDESCRS
             NEG-HDESCRS
             HNAME))]
    (COND
      [MGDS (MSG T)
       (MAPC
         (F:L (RULE) (ADD-GR (CAR RULE) (CADR RULE) T))
         (TRIM-ALL-TRAILING-DIGITS MGDS))
       (MSG O T (T 3) "Least-disjunction was successful." T)
       T]
      [T (MSG O T (T 3)
            "Least-disjunction was not successul!" T)
         (PUSH
           \UNASSIMILATED-DISJUNCTIONS
           (LIST POS-HDESCRS NEG-HDESCRS HNAME))
         NIL]))))

(DE BACK-PROPAGATE (SOLUTION-SEQUENCE PAT)
  {;; Any disjunctions along the way are incorporated into
      the CDL. Thus it is okay to assume that a single pattern
      gets returned at any level. Thinking here is that if the
      CRITIC ordains a solution sequence as preferred, then
      the CRITIC would also ordain any tail of that sequence
      as preferred. Therefore, any amount of back-propagation
      that can be done is useful.}
  (AND SOLUTION-SEQUENCE
    (COND
      [(EQ (LENGTH SOLUTION-SEQUENCE) 1)
```

```
            (WITH [(X (MAPCONC (F:L (Y)
                        (LIST
                          (CP-BACK-PROP
                            (CAR SOLUTION-SEQUENCE)
                            (LIST Y 'NO-BINDINGS))))
                          (CP-INTERSECT
                            (CAR SOLUTION-SEQUENCE)
                            PAT
                            '(NO-INTO-INTERSECTIONS)))))]
              (COND
                [(CDR X)
                 (MSG
                   "Back propagation is a disjunction"
                   (E (HELPME)))]
                [T (CAR X)])))]
            [T (WITH [(BPVAL
                        (BACK-PROPAGATE
                          (CDR SOLUTION-SEQUENCE)
                          PAT))]
              (COND
                [(EQ BPVAL 'APPLY-OP-FAILS)        BPVAL]
                [T (WITH [(X (MAPCONC (F:L (Y)
                              (LIST
                                (CP-BACK-PROP
                                  (CAR SOLUTION-SEQUENCE)
                                  (LIST
                                    Y
                                    'THROW-AWAY-BINDINGS))))
                                (CP-INTERSECT
                                  (CAR SOLUTION-SEQUENCE)
                                  (CAR BPVAL)
                                  NIL)))]
                      (COND
                        [(CDR X)
                         (MSG "Back propagation is a disjunction"
                           (E (HELPME)))]
                        [T (CAR X)])))])))])))

(DE CONSTRAINT-BACKPROP (SOLUTION-SEQUENCE)
  (MSG O T (T 3)
    "Attempting revision of CDL using "
    "constraint-propagation."
    T)
  (WITH [(BPVAL
```

```
            (BACK-PROPAGATE SOLUTION-SEQUENCE 'AEXPR))]
    (COND
      [(EQ BPVAL 'APPLY-OP-FAILS)
       (MSG 0 T (T 3)
         "Unable to complete constraint-propagation"
         T)]
      [BPVAL
       (MSG 0 T (T 3)
         "Constraint-propagation was successful." T)
       T]
      [T (MSG 0 T (T 3)
         "Constraint-propagation returns empty-set.")]))))
(DE CP-BACK-PROP (SOL-STEP PAT)
  (COND
    [(EQ PAT 'APPLY-OP-FAILS)          PAT]
    [T
     (WITH [(OPNAME (CAADDR SOL-STEP))
            (FB
             (COND
               [(INP '--> SOL-STEP)
                (FIND-BINDINGS SOL-STEP)]
               [(INP '==> SOL-STEP)
                (FIND-BINDINGS SOL-STEP)]
               [T
                {;; Will already be bindings if called by
                    undo-approx-apply}
                (CADR (CADDR SOL-STEP))]))
            RMAPS]
       (SETQ RMAPS
         (MATCH (GET OPNAME 'RHS) (CAR PAT) '(NO-AMB-DERS)))
       (COND
         [RMAPS
          (WITH [(RPATS
                  (MAPCONC (F:L (MAP)
                      {;; Would normally use APPLY-OP here
                       except that we need to keep the
                       binding list for the bindings check.
                       So we do what APPLY-OP does (see
                       APPLY-OP for similarity).}
                      (WITH [(LB (FIND-BINDINGS MAP))]
                        (WITH [(RB
                                (EVAL
                                 (GET
```

```
                               OPNAME
                               'BACKWARD)))]
              (COND
                [(EQ RB 'APPLY-OP-FAILS)
                 (MSG O T (T 3)
          "Unable to back-propagate via backward "
                      OPNAME
                      T)
                 (NCONS RB)]
                [T
                 (WITH [(BP
                            (REWRITE-MAP
                              MAP
                              LB
                              RB
                              (GET
                                 OPNAME
                                 'LHS)))
                        BB]
                      (SETQ BB
                        (APPEND
                          LB RB
                          (ADDITIONAL-BINDINGS
                            (UNION LB RB)
                            (GET OPNAME 'LHS))))
                      (AND
                        (EVERY (F:L (FB*)
                            (SOME (F:L (BB*)
                                   (AND
                                     (EQ
                                        (CAR BB*)
                                        (CAR FB*))
                                     (MATCH
                                        (CDR BB*)
                                        (CDR FB*)
                                        '(NO-AMB-DERS))))
                                  BB))
                               FB)
                        (NCONS (LIST BP BB))))])))))
             RMAPS))]
       (MSG O T (T 3) "Back-propagation via backward "
         OPNAME T (T 5) "Result:"
         (E (SPRINT RPATS 15)) T)
       (COND
```

```
                [RPATS
                 (COND
                   [(EQ (LENGTH RPATS) 1) (CAR RPATS)]
                   [T (MSG O "Back-propagation is a disjunction, "
                           "halting via (HELPME)"  T)
                      (HELPME)])])]
                [T (MSG O T (T 3) "All propagated bindings were "
                      "inconsistent with original forward binding"
                      T)])))]
          [T (MSG O "Range of " (CAR PAT)
             " does not match " PAT T)])))])))

(DE CP-INTERSECT (SOL-STEP PAT FLAGS)
  (WITH [(OPNAME (CAADDR SOL-STEP)) RHS INTS]
    (SETQ RHS (GET OPNAME 'RHS))
    (MSG O T (T 3) "Intersecting range of "
      OPNAME " and pattern" (T 5)
      "Range:" (E (SPRINT RHS 15)) (T 5)
      "Pattern:" (E (SPRINT PAT 15)) (T 5)
      "Result:")
    (SETQ INTS (INTERSECT RHS PAT FLAGS))
    (MSG (E (SPRINT INTS 15)) T)
    (OR INTS
      (MSG O "Range of " OPNAME " does not intersect " PAT T))))

(DE CREATE-DISJUNCTION (PATS)
  {;; PATS is a set of patterns which is intended to be
      describable in the CDL.}
  (AND \DEBUG-LEAST-DISJUNCTION
    (MSG O "Extracted disjunction is:" (E (SPRINT PATS 3)) T))
  (WITH [(MAPS*
           (MAPCAR (F:L (PAT) (MATCH 'ANY PAT NIL)) PATS))]
    (WITH [(MG-PATS
             (MAXPATTERNS (CREATE-DISJUNCTION* MAPS* NIL)))
           (NEW-TERM (NEWSYM))]
      (AND \DEBUG-LEAST-DISJUNCTION
        (MSG O "More general existing terms are:"
          (E (SPRINT MG-PATS 3)) T))
      {;; We can put together the new grammar rules here.
          For now assuming these are always patterns. May have
          to fix this later to work with FUNs as well.}
      {;; Splice new language term as more general than
          disjuncts and more specific than those maximally
```

```
            specific expressions in the existing language which
            already cover the disjuncts.}
       (COND
         [MG-PATS
          (NCONC
            (MAPCAR (F:L (MG-PAT)
                    (LIST (CONS 'PAT MG-PAT) (CONS 'PAT NEW-TERM)))
              MG-PATS)
            (MAPCAR (F:L (PAT)
                    (LIST (CONS 'PAT NEW-TERM) (CONS 'PAT PAT)))
              PATS))]
         [T (MSG O "MG-PATS null in CREATE-DISJUNCTION"
            (E (HELPME)))]))))


(DE CREATE-DISJUNCTION* (MAP-GROUPS ORG)
  {;; This is similar to MSU except that there may be more
       than two disjuncts. Also, there is no lhs to limit the
       generality.}
  {;; Look at the map groups in parallel to find
       generalizations in the existing language which are more
       general than the disjuncts. Such generalizations will be
       made to point to the new description in the language,
       which in turn will point to the disjuncts.}
  (COND
    [(SOME (F:L (GR) (NULL GR)) MAP-GROUPS)
     {;; If a map-group has become NIL then stop with
          failure.}
     NIL]
    [(SOME
        (F:L (GR)
          (SOME
            (F:L (MAP*)
              (OR
                (ATOM MAP*)
                (NOT (MEMQ (CAR MAP*) '(--> ==>)))))
            GR))
        MAP-GROUPS)
     {;; If something in one of the map-groups is no
          longer mapped, then stop.}
     (NCONS ORG)]
    [T
     {;; Am ignoring list decomposition. I think that is
          okay, but should think about this. The assumptions
```

```
                  that are valid at this point should be spelled out.}
          (WITH [F1 F2 (TOP (CADAAR MAP-GROUPS))]
            (MAPC
              (F:L (MAP-GROUP)
                (WITH [F3 F4]
                  (MAPC
                    (F:L (MAP*)
                      (COND
                        [(EQ (CADR MAP*) TOP)
                         (PUSH F3 (CADDR MAP*))]
                        [T (PUSH F4 (CADDR MAP*))]))
                    MAP-GROUP)
                  (PUSH F1 (REVERSE F3))
                  (PUSH F2 (REVERSE F4))))
              MAP-GROUPS)
            (COND
              [(AND (MEMQ NIL F2) (MEMQ NIL F1))
               {;; If unable to get next level of mapgroups,
                  then done}
               (NCONS ORG)]
              [T
               (NCONC
                 (CREATE-DISJUNCTION* (REVERSE F1) TOP)
                 (CREATE-DISJUNCTION* (REVERSE F2) TOP))])))])))

(DE LOOKUP-FUN (ARGDEF CDL-NODES)
  (AND CDL-NODES
    (WITH [(NODE-VAL (EVAL (CAR CDL-NODES)))]
      (COND
        [(EQUAL
           (TRIM-ALL-TRAILING-DIGITS (CAR NODE-VAL))
           ARGDEF)
         (CADR NODE-VAL)]
        [T (LOOKUP-FUN ARGDEF (CDR CDL-NODES))]))))

(DE LOOKUP-OR-MAKE (MG MS MG-FOR-NEW-TERM)
  {;; Return term which corresponds to indicated instance
     test. If no such test is found, add it to the CDL.}
  (COND
    [(MATCH MG MG-FOR-NEW-TERM '(NO-INTO-MAPS))          MG]
    [T
     (WITH [(ARGDEF
              (LIST 'FUN 'LAMBDA '(LVAR)
                (LIST 'MATCH
```

```
                    (LIST 'QUOTE MG) MS
                    (LIST 'QUOTE '(NO-INTO-MAPS))))))]
       (WITH [(LOOKUP-VAL
                (LOOKUP-FUN
                  (TRIM-ALL-TRAILING-DIGITS ARGDEF)
                  (CAR \CDL)))]
          (COND
            [LOOKUP-VAL
              {;; Here we build in assumption that instance
                 test function is more specific than exactly
                 one item in language.}
              (CAR LOOKUP-VAL)]
            [T
              (WITH [(NEW-TERM (NEWSYM))]
                (ADD-GR (CONS 'PAT NEW-TERM) ARGDEF T)
                (ADD-GR
                  (CONS 'PAT MG-FOR-NEW-TERM)
                  (CONS 'PAT NEW-TERM)
                  T)
                NEW-TERM)])))])))

(DE MOST-GENERAL-DISJUNCTIONS (POS-HDESCRS NEG-HDESCRS HNAME)
  {;; POS-HDESCRS is the least disjunction. Here
      we want to identify the most general disjunction(s?)
      which can be used to create a new term in the CDL.}
  (WITH [(LHS
           (GET (GET HNAME 'RECOMMENDED-OPERATOR) 'LHS))]
    (MOST-GENERAL-DISJUNCTIONS*
      (MAPCONC
        (F:L (H)
          (MAPCAR
            (F:L (MAP)
              (UNMAP-MOST-SPECIFIC
                (CAR (REVERSE (FIND-MAP-EMBEDDINGS MAP)))))
            (GENMAPS LHS (CAR H) '(NO-AMB-DERS) (CADR H))))
        POS-HDESCRS)
      (MAPCONC
        (F:L (H)
          (MAPCAR
            (F:L (MAP)
              (UNMAP-MOST-SPECIFIC
                (CAR (REVERSE (FIND-MAP-EMBEDDINGS MAP)))))
            (GENMAPS LHS (CAR H) '(NO-AMB-DERS) (CADR H))))
        NEG-HDESCRS))))
```

```
(DE MOST-GENERAL-DISJUNCTIONS* (POS-PATS NEG-PATS)
  {;; POS-PATS and NEG-PATS are patterns which can be
      matched onto by the lhs of the operator. It is okay
      therefore to do some parallel decomposition looking for
      simplest disjunctions.}
  (AND POS-PATS NEG-PATS
    (COND
      [(SOME (F:L (POS-PAT) (ATOM POS-PAT)) POS-PATS)
       {;; If a CAR of some POS-PAT is an atom, then don't
           try any further decomposition.}
       (COND
         [(SOME
            (F:L (POS-PAT)
              (SOME
                (F:L (NEG-PAT)
                  (MATCH POS-PAT NEG-PAT '(NO-AMB-DERS)))
                NEG-PATS))
            POS-PATS)
          {;; If any POS-PAT matches any NEG-PAT then no
              disjunction possible.}
          NIL]
         [T
          {;; Otherwise, the set of POS-PATS is a
              consistent disjunction.}
          (CREATE-DISJUNCTION POS-PATS)])]
      [T
       {;; Try parallel decomposition to look for a
           simpler disjunction.}
       (WITH [(DEEPER
                (MAPCONC (FUNCTION MOST-GENERAL-DISJUNCTIONS*)
                  (EVAL
                    (CONS
                      'MAPCAR
                      (CONS
                        '(FUNCTION LIST)
                        (MAPCAR
                          (F:L (PAT)
                            (LIST 'QUOTE PAT))
                          POS-PATS))))
                  (EVAL
                    (CONS
                      'MAPCAR
                      (CONS
```

```
                    '(FUNCTION LIST)
                    (MAPCAR
                      (F:L (PAT)
                        (LIST 'QUOTE PAT))
                      NEG-PATS)))))))]
            (OR DEEPER (CREATE-DISJUNCTION POS-PATS)))])))

(DE REVISE-CDL (HNAME INST INST-CLASSIFICATION)
  (COND
    [(OR
        (CONSTRAINT-BACKPROP
          (SOME (F:L (INST*) (EQUAL INST INST*))
            (SORT \PLUS-INSTANCES)))
        (LEAST-DISJUNCTION
          (CONS (CONS INST-CLASSIFICATION INST)
                (GET HNAME 'EVIDENCE))
          HNAME))
      {;; If one of these revsision processes actually
          revised the CDL, then success.}
      (MSG O T (T 3)
        "CDL revised, will reprocess all training "
        "instances for this heuristic." T)
      {;; Actually, it is necessary to reprocess instances
          for ALL the heuristics. Otherwise, the S and G sets
          may be more converged than would be the case via the
          candidate elimination algorithm. The code does not
          currently redo the other heuristics, bug!!}
      (WITH [(INSTS-TO-REPROCESS
                (CONS (CONS INST-CLASSIFICATION INST)
                      (GET HNAME 'EVIDENCE)))
               \CDL-REVISION-SWITCH]
        {;; Reset evidence to NIL.}
        (REMPROPS HNAME '(EVIDENCE GS SS))
        {;; Now reprocess the instances. Note that we turn
            off the revision mechanism. If the revision process
            has erred in some unforseen way, we don't want to
            get stuck in infinite recursion.}
        (PROCESS-INSTS HNAME INSTS-TO-REPROCESS)
        'PROCESSING-FINISHED-AFTER-CDL-REVISION)]
    [T {;; Otherwise return NIL for failure. Coming here is
          a serious failure.}
      (MSG O T (T 3) "Unable to revise CDL; ")]))

(DE LD1 (DISJUNCTION NEG-HDESCRS HNAME)
```

```
{;; Does a search on combinations of D for disjunctions
    which cover some of the positive instances and none of
    the negative instances. LEAST-HDESCRS should me used to
    filter out subsumed disjuncts.}
(AND DISJUNCTION
  (COND
    [(ATOM DISJUNCTION) {;; D cannot be an atom} (HELPME)]
    [(CDR DISJUNCTION)
     {;; List is at least two elements, so try to
        generalize.}
     (WITH [(NEW-DISJUNCT
             (LD2 (CAR DISJUNCTION) (CADR DISJUNCTION)
               NEG-HDESCRS HNAME))]
       (COND
         [NEW-DISJUNCT
          (COND
            [(CDDR DISJUNCTION)
             (NCONC
               (LD1
                 (CONS NEW-DISJUNCT (CDDR DISJUNCTION))
                 NEG-HDESCRS
                 HNAME)
               (LD1
                 (CONS (CAR DISJUNCTION)
                       (CDDR DISJUNCTION))
                 NEG-HDESCRS HNAME))]
            [T
             (LD1
               (CONS NEW-DISJUNCT (CDDR DISJUNCTION))
               NEG-HDESCRS HNAME)])]
         [T
          (LD1
            (CONS (CAR DISJUNCTION) (CDDR DISJUNCTION))
            NEG-HDESCRS HNAME)])))]
    [T DISJUNCTION])))
(DE LD2 (HDESCR1 HDESCR2 NEG-HDESCRS HNAME)
  {;; Returns a single (design choice, could be to weak)
     hdescr generalization of HDESCR1 and HDESCR2 iff it does
     not cover any of the NEG-HDESCRS. Note that by choosing
     exactly one (if several were possible), we may miss some
     disjuncts which might suggest more favorable language
     changes?}
  (WITH [(NH
```

```
        (SUBSET
          (F:L (NEWH)
            (NOT
              (SOME
                (F:L (NEGH)
                  (MORE-SPECIFIC-HEURISTIC NEGH NEWH))
                NEG-HDESCRS)))
          (WITH [(LHS
                   (GET
                     (GET HNAME 'RECOMMENDED-OPERATOR)
                     'LHS))]
            (MSU-HDESCRS
              HDESCR1
              (GENMAPS LHS (CAR HDESCR1)
                NIL (CADR HDESCR1))
              HDESCR2
              (GENMAPS LHS (CAR HDESCR2)
                NIL (CADR HDESCR2))
              HNAME))))]
    (AND NH (CAR NH))))

(DE LEAST-DISJUNCTION (INSTS HNAME)
  {;; The disjunction of the pos-insts must be consistent
   (assuming a consistent trainer), so we'll start with
   that disjunction and then try to make it as general as
   possible in the present language. That least
   disjunction will then be used to determine a change to
   the language.}
  {;; Currently written to use exactly one disjunction for
   the language change.}
  (MSG O T (T 3)
    "Attempting revision of CDL using least-disjunction." T)
  (WITH [POS-HDESCRS NEG-HDESCRS]
    (MAPC
      (F:L (INST)
        (COND
          [(EQ (CAR INST) 'POS)
           (PUSH POS-HDESCRS (INST-TO-HDESCR (CDR INST)))]
          [(EQ (CAR INST) 'NEG)
           (PUSH NEG-HDESCRS (INST-TO-HDESCR (CDR INST)))]
          [T
           (MSG O "**** instance has bad label "
                "in LEAST-DISJUNCTION: " INST T)]))
      INSTS)
```

```
(ASSIMILATE-DISJUNCTION
  (LEAST-HDESCRS
   (MAPCON (F:L (D) (LD1 D NEG-HDESCRS HNAME))
     POS-HDESCRS))
  NEG-HDESCRS
  HNAME)))
```

```
(DE TEST NIL (CONSTRAINT-BACKPROP (SORT \PLUS-INSTANCES)))
```

```
(DV \DEBUG-CP T)
```

```
(DV \DEBUG-LEAST-DISJUNCTION T)
```

```
(DV \UNASSIMILATED-DISJUNCTIONS NIL)
```

A.2   Grammar

These functions define and provide operations on the grammar. The grammar is structured as a graph of nodes (atoms). For each, there is a list of the more general nodes, a list of the more specific nodes, and an associated pattern or recognition predicate.

```
(DE NEWSYM NIL
  (READLIST
   (NCONC (NCONS "N")
     (AEXPLODEC (INCR \NEWSYM-COUNTER)) (NCONS "S"))))
```

```
(SETQ \NEWSYM-COUNTER 0)
```

```
(DE ADD-GR (L1 R1 PRINT-FLAG)
  {;; Modify \CDL and current data structure to include
     new grammar rule.}
  (AND PRINT-FLAG
    (MSG O (T 5) "Adding grammar rule to CDL:"
      (T 7) L1 " ==> " R1 T))
  (AND (CONSP L1) (CONSP R1)
    (COND
      [(AND (EQ (CAR L1) 'PAT) (CONSP (CDR L1)))
      {;; Context-sensitive rule.}
      (RPLACA
        (CDDDR \CDL)
        (CONS (LIST (CDR L1) (CDR R1)) (CADDDR \CDL)))]
      [T
```

```
           (WITH [(LNAM (FIND-OR-MAKE-GNODE-NAME L1))
                  (RNAM (FIND-OR-MAKE-GNODE-NAME R1))]
             (WITH [(LVAL (EVAL LNAM)) (RVAL (EVAL RNAM))]
               (RPLACA (CDDR LVAL) (CONS RNAM (CADDR LVAL)))
               (RPLACA (CDR RVAL) (CONS LNAM (CADR RVAL)))))]))))

(DE FIND-GNODE-NAME (PAT NODE-NAMES)
  (AND NODE-NAMES
    (COND
      [(EQUAL PAT (CDAR (EVAL (CAR NODE-NAMES))))
       (CAR NODE-NAMES)]
      [T (FIND-GNODE-NAME PAT (CDR NODE-NAMES))]])))

(DE FIND-NODE (PAT)
  (COND
    [(BOUNDP PAT) (EVAL PAT)]
    [T
     (WITH [(TPAT
              (SOME
                (F:L (NODENAME)
                  (WITH [(NVAL (EVAL NODENAME))]
                    (AND (EQ (CAAR NVAL) 'PAT)
                         (EQUAL (CDAR NVAL) PAT))))
                (CADDR \CDL)))]
       (AND TPAT (EVAL (CAR TPAT))))]))

(DE FIND-OR-MAKE-GNODE-NAME (PAT)
  {;; If a node exists in the grammar which corresponds to
   PAT, then returns that, else creates such a node and
   returns the new name.}
  (COND
    [(ATOM PAT)
     (MSG 0
       "**** illegal PAT in FIND-OR-MAKE-GNODE-NAME is: "
       PAT T)]
    [(EQ (CAR PAT) 'PAT)
     (COND
       [(OR (CONSP (CDR PAT)) (NUMBERP (CDR PAT)))
        (OR (FIND-GNODE-NAME (CDR PAT) (CADDR \CDL))
            (WITH [(NAM (NEWSYM))]
              (SET NAM (LIST PAT NIL NIL))
              (RPLACA (CDDR \CDL) (CONS NAM (CADDR \CDL)))
              NAM))]
       [T (COND
```

```
                 [(BOUNDP (CDR PAT)) (CDR PAT)]
                 [T (SET (CDR PAT) (LIST PAT NIL NIL))
                    (RPLACA (CDR \CDL)
                            (CONS (CDR PAT) (CADR \CDL)))
                    (CDR PAT)])])]
       [(EQ (CAR PAT) 'FUN)
        (OR (FIND-GNODE-NAME (CDR PAT) (CAR \CDL))
            (WITH [(NAM (NEWSYM))]
              (SET NAM (LIST PAT NIL NIL))
              (RPLACA \CDL (CONS NAM (CAR \CDL)))
              NAM))]
       [T (MSG 0
          "**** illegal PAT in FIND-OR-MAKE-GNODE-NAME is: "
          PAT T)]))

(SETQ \CDL (LIST NIL NIL NIL NIL))

(DV \GRAMMAR
  (((PAT . +*) (PAT . +))
   ((PAT . +*) (PAT . *))
   ((PAT . +-) (PAT . +))
   ((PAT . +-) (PAT . -))
   ((PAT . A:FFR) (PAT FFR A:FFR))
   ((PAT . A:FFR) (PAT FR A:FR))
   ((PAT . A:FR)
    (FUN LAMBDA (LVAR
      (AND (ATOM LVAR) (NOT (NUMBERP LVAR))
           (NOT (INP LVAR \CDL)))))
   ((PAT . AEXPR) (PAT FR A:FR))
   ((PAT . AEXPR) (PAT . A:FR))
   ((PAT . AEXPR) (PAT &&OP AEXPR AEXPR))
   ((PAT . AEXPR) (PAT . C))
   ((PAT . ANY) (PAT . IEXPR))
   ((PAT . ANY) (PAT . FFR))
   ((PAT . ANY) (PAT . FR))
   ((PAT . ANY) (PAT . COMB))
   ((PAT . C) (PAT . CPRIM))
   ((PAT . C) (PAT &&OP C C))
   ((PAT . CNM) (PAT . CNMZ))
   ((PAT . CNM) (PAT . KNM))
   ((PAT . CNMZ) (PAT . R))
   ((PAT . CNMZ) (PAT . KNMZ))
   ((PAT . CNZ) (PAT . KNZ))
   ((PAT . CNZ) (PAT . CNMZ))
```

```
((PAT . COMB) (PAT . &&OP))
((PAT . COMB) (PAT . ~))
((PAT . CPRIM) (PAT . CNM))
((PAT . CPRIM) (PAT . K))
((PAT . CPRIM) (PAT . CNZ))
((PAT . EXPON) (PAT . LN))
((PAT . EXPON) (PAT . EXP))
((PAT . FFR) (PAT . INT))
((PAT . FFR) (PAT . DER))
((PAT . FR) (PAT . PRIM))
((PAT . FR) (PAT COMB FR FR))
((PAT . IEXPR) (PAT . A:FFR))
((PAT . IEXPR) (PAT . AEXPR))
((PAT . IEXPR) (PAT &&OP IEXPR IEXPR))
((PAT . K) (PAT . KNM))
((PAT . K) (PAT . KNZ))
((PAT . KNM) (PAT . KNMZ))
((PAT . KNM) (PAT . 0))
((PAT . KNMZ)
 (FUN LAMBDA (LVAR)
   (AND (NUMBERP LVAR) (EQUAL LVAR (FIX LVAR))
        (NOT (MEMQ LVAR (QUOTE (0 -1)))))))
((PAT . KNZ) (PAT . KNMZ))
((PAT . KNZ) (PAT . -1))
((PAT . MONOM) (PAT . C))
((PAT . MONOM) (PAT * C ID))
((PAT . MONOM) (PAT ^ ID K))
((PAT . MONOM) (PAT . ID))
((PAT . MONOM) (PAT * C (^ ID K)))
((PAT . &&OP) (PAT . +-))
((PAT . &&OP) (PAT . +*))
((PAT . &&OP) (PAT . \))
((PAT . &&OP) (PAT . ^))
((PAT . POLY) (PAT . MONOM))
((PAT . POLY) (PAT +- POLY MONOM))
((PAT . PRIM) (PAT . POLY))
((PAT . PRIM) (PAT . TRANSC))
((PAT . R)
 (FUN LAMBDA (LVAR)
   (OR (AND (NUMBERP LVAR) (NOT (EQUAL LVAR (FIX LVAR))))
       (EQ LVAR (QUOTE E)))))
((PAT . TRANSC) (PAT . ABS))
((PAT . TRANSC) (PAT . TRIG))
((PAT . TRANSC) (PAT . EXPON))
```

```
      ((PAT . TRIG) (PAT . SEC))
      ((PAT . TRIG) (PAT . COT))
      ((PAT . TRIG) (PAT . CSC))
      ((PAT . TRIG) (PAT . SIN))
      ((PAT . TRIG) (PAT . COS))
      ((PAT . TRIG) (PAT . TAN))))

(MAPC (F:L (RULE)
    (APPLY (F:L (LHS RHS) (ADD-GR LHS RHS NIL)) RULE))
  \GRAMMAR)
```

A.3 Intersection

This section contains the functions that define the intersection of two descriptions. The top-level function is INTERSECT.

```
(DE INTERSECT (P1 P2 FLAGS)
  {;; P1 and P2 are patterns. Returns a list of least
      specific intersections of P1 and P2.}
  {;; Any flags given here are passed along to calls to
      MATCH. Some of these flags may not make sense, but no
      need to impose arbitrary restrictions here, so be
      careful! One flag specifically recognized within
      INTERSECT is NO-INTO-INTERSECTIONS. It is analogous to
      the NO-INTO-MAPS for MATCH. If the flag is specified,
      then no attempt will be made to intersect one pattern
      with a subpart of the other pattern.}
  {;; We always want to (in effect) be using the
      NO-CF-SUBMATCHES flag. That is, we never want to
      mis-parse something because of ignoring the context in
      which something appeared. We use portions of MATCH below
      where that check is normally done, so do it here,
      ALWAYS, no option.}
  (LEASTPATTERNS
    (SUBSET (F:L (P*)
        (MATCH 'ANY P* '(NO-INTO-MAPS NO-AMB-DERS)))
      (NCONC
        (INTERSECT* P1 P2 FLAGS (CONS NIL NIL) NIL)
        (INTERSECT* P2 P1 FLAGS (CONS NIL NIL) NIL)))))

(DE INTERSECT* (P1 P2 FLAGS P1CP2C COMPARISONS)
  (AND P1 P2
    (SETQ P1CP2C
```

```
      (CONS
        (OR (CAR P1CP2C) (UNTAG-TRIM P1))
        (OR (CDR P1CP2C) (UNTAG-TRIM P2))))
    (WITH [(INTS
            (INTERSECT-ONTO P1 P2 FLAGS
                   P1CP2C COMPARISONS))]
      (COND
        [(MEMQ 'NO-INTO-INTERSECTIONS FLAGS)            INTS]
        [INTS]
        [T
         (LEASTPATTERNS
          (CDR
           (INTERSECT-INTO P1 P2 FLAGS
                  P1CP2C COMPARISONS)))])))))

(DE INTERSECT-ATOM-ONTO (P1 P2 FLAGS P1CP2C COMPARISONS)
  (WITH [(NODE (FIND-NODE (CAR P1CP2C)))]
    (AND NODE
      (LEASTPATTERNS
        (MAPCONC
          (F:L (NODENAM)
            (WITH [(NVAL (EVAL NODENAM))]
              (COND
                [NVAL
                 (COND
                   [(EQ (CAAR NVAL) 'PAT)
                    (COND
                      [(MEMBER (CONS (CDAR NVAL) (CDR P1CP2C))
                         COMPARISONS)
                       NIL]
                      [T
                       (INTERSECT-ONTO (CDAR NVAL) P2
                         FLAGS (CONS NIL (CDR P1CP2C))
                         (CONS
                           (CONS (CDAR NVAL) (CDR P1CP2C))
                           COMPARISONS))])]
                   [(EQ (CAAR NVAL) 'FUN)
                    (AND
                      (APPLY (CDAR NVAL) (NCONS (CDR P1CP2C)))
                      (NCONS (CDR P1CP2C)))]
                   [T (MSG 0
                      "Ill-formed grammar rule at "
                      NODENAM T)])]
                [T (MSG 0
```

```
                    "Ill-formed grammar rule at "
                    NODENAM T)])))
          (CADDR NODE))))))

(DE INTERSECT-CS-ONTO (P1 P2 FLAGS P1CP2C COMPARISONS)
  {;; P1 is a list. If there is a context sensitive rule
     whose RHS intersects P2, then anything (e.g. P1) that
     matches LHS also intersects P2.}
  (MAPCONC
    (F:L (CSRULE)
      (WITH [(IS
               (INTERSECT-ONTO (CDR CSRULE) P2
                 FLAGS (CONS NIL (CDR P1CP2C))
                 COMPARISONS))]
        (AND IS
          (MATCH-ONTO P1 (CAR CSRULE) FLAGS
            (CAR P1CP2C)NIL)
          IS)))
    (CADDDR \CDL)))

(DE INTERSECT-INTO (P1 P2 FLAGS P1CP2C COMPARISONS)
  {;; Return an intersection where P1 can intersect a
     subpart of P2. Note that this is not symmetric, so a
     caller will want to use this twice. In addition, this
     code is made simpler by assuming the first element in
     the returned list contains no intersection. So, the
     original caller of this function should use CDR of what
     is returned.}
  (AND P2
    (COND
      [(ATOM (CDR P1CP2C)) {;; Atom not decomposable.}
          (NCONS P2)]
      [T
       (WITH [(TCAR
                (CONS
                  (CAR (CDR P1CP2C))
                  (INTERSECT* P1 (CAR (CDR P1CP2C))
                    FLAGS (CONS (CAR P1CP2C) NIL)
                    COMPARISONS)))
              (TCDR
               (CONS
                 (CDR (CDR P1CP2C))
                 (INTERSECT* P1 (CDR (CDR P1CP2C))
                   FLAGS (CONS (CAR P1CP2C) NIL)
```

```
                          COMPARISONS))))]
             {;; If TCDR then two lists to join are (old1 a b
                c) and (old2 x y z). Join old1 to everything in
                the second list, and join everything in first
                list (except old1) to old2. If TCDR is NIL then
                join everything in first list to NIL.}
             (COND
               [TCDR
                (NCONC
                   (MAPCAR (F:L (TCDR*) (CONS (CAR TCAR) TCDR*))
                      TCDR)
                   (MAPCAR (F:L (TCAR*) (CONS TCAR* (CAR TCDR)))
                      (CDR TCAR)))]
               [T (MAPCAR (FUNCTION NCONS) TCAR)])))]))))

(DE INTERSECT-LIST-ONTO (P1 P2 FLAGS P1CP2C COMPARISONS)
  {;; Known that length of P1 same as length of P2.}
  (WITH [TEMP]
    (AND
      (EVERY
        (F:L (P1* P2*)
          (WITH [(TINTS
                    (INTERSECT-ONTO P1* P2* FLAGS
                       (CONS NIL NIL) COMPARISONS))]
            (AND TINTS (PUSH TEMP TINTS))))
        (CAR P1CP2C)
        (CDR P1CP2C))
      (LEASTPATTERNS (ALL-COMBINATIONS (DREVERSE TEMP))))))

(DE INTERSECT-ONTO (P1 P2 FLAGS P1CP2C COMPARISONS)
  (AND P1 P2
    (SETQ P1CP2C
      (CONS
        (OR (CAR P1CP2C) (UNTAG-TRIM P1))
        (OR (CDR P1CP2C) (UNTAG-TRIM P2))))
    (COND
      [(MATCH-ONTO P1 P2 FLAGS (CAR P1CP2C) (CDR P1CP2C))
       (NCONS P2)]
      [(MATCH-ONTO P2 P1 FLAGS (CDR P1CP2C) (CAR P1CP2C))
       (NCONS P1)]
      [(AND (ATOM (CAR P1CP2C)) (ATOM (CDR P1CP2C)))
       (OR
         (INTERSECT-ATOM-ONTO P1 P2 FLAGS
           P1CP2C COMPARISONS)
```

```
        (INTERSECT-ATOM-ONTO P2 P1 FLAGS
           P1CP2C COMPARISONS))]
    [(AND (ATOM (CAR P1CP2C)) (NOT (ATOM (CDR P1CP2C))))
     (OR
       (INTERSECT-ATOM-ONTO P1 P2 FLAGS P1CP2C
          COMPARISONS)
       (INTERSECT-CS-ONTO P2 P1 FLAGS P1CP2C
          COMPARISONS))]
    [(AND (ATOM (CDR P1CP2C)) (NOT (ATOM (CAR P1CP2C))))
     (OR
       (INTERSECT-ATOM-ONTO P2 P1 FLAGS P1CP2C
          COMPARISONS)
       (INTERSECT-CS-ONTO P1 P2 FLAGS P1CP2C
          COMPARISONS))]
    [(EQUAL (LENGTH (CAR P1CP2C)) (LENGTH (CDR P1CP2C)))
     (INTERSECT-LIST-ONTO P1 P2 FLAGS P1CP2C
        COMPARISONS)])))
```

A.4   Match

This section contains the MATCH function. MATCH returns a list of derivation trees showing how the more general pattern MG matches the more specific pattern MS.

```
(DE MATCH (MG MS FLAGS)
  (WITH [(MAPS (MATCH* MG MS FLAGS NIL NIL))]
    (COND
      [(MEMQ 'NO-CF-SUBMATCHES FLAGS)
       {;; Filter out context-free submatches. This is
          expensive, so only use it if necessary. It can
          happen that something like 'fr will match something
          like '3 in some context where '3 is NOT an 'fr but
          is an 'expr. This is where we filter out such
          things if they are specifically not wanted.}
       (SUBSET
         (F:L (MAP*)
           (MATCH 'ANY (UNMAP-MOST-GENERAL MAP*)
             '(NO-INTO-MAPS NO-AMB-DERS)))
         MAPS)]
      [T MAPS])))

(DE MATCH* (MG MS FLAGS MG-CLEAN MS-CLEAN)
  {;; Return a list of maps from MG to MS as per FLAGS.}
```

```
(AND MG MS
  (OR MG-CLEAN (SETQ MG-CLEAN (UNTAG-TRIM MG)))
  (OR MS-CLEAN (SETQ MS-CLEAN (UNTAG-TRIM MS)))
  (WITH [(MAPS
            (MATCH-ONTO MG MS FLAGS MG-CLEAN MS-CLEAN))]
      (COND
        [(MEMQ 'NO-INTO-MAPS FLAGS)
         {;; If submatches are not wanted then stop.}
         MAPS]
        [T
         {;; If submatches are wanted then add those to
            what we have already.}
         (NCONC MAPS
            (CDR (MATCH-INTO MG MS FLAGS
                             MG-CLEAN MS-CLEAN)))])))))

(DE MATCH-ATOM-ONTO (MG MS FLAGS MG-CLEAN MS-CLEAN)
  {;; This function is a primitive for MATCH-ONTO. Beware
     using it independantly.}
  (WITH [(NODE (FIND-NODE MG-CLEAN))]
    (AND NODE
      (MAPCONC
        (F:L (NODENAM)
          (WITH [(NVAL (EVAL NODENAM))]
            (COND
              [NVAL
                (COND
                  [(EQ (CAAR NVAL) 'PAT)
                   (MAPCAR
                     (F:L (MAP) (LIST '--> MG MAP))
                     (MATCH-ONTO (CDAR NVAL) MS
                       FLAGS NIL MS-CLEAN))]
                  [(EQ (CAAR NVAL) 'FUN)
                   (AND (APPLY (CDAR NVAL) (NCONS MS-CLEAN))
                        (NCONS (LIST '--> MG MS)))]
                  [T (MSG 0 "Ill-formed grammar rule at "
                       NODENAM T)])]
              [T (MSG 0 "Ill-formed grammar rule at "
                   NODENAM T)])))
        (CADDR NODE)))))

(DE MATCH-CS-ONTO (MG MS FLAGS MG-CLEAN MS-CLEAN)
  {;; Return maps from MG onto MS using any
     context-sensitive grammar rules whose right-hand-side
```

```
      matches MS as per FLAGS.}
  (MAPCONC
    (F:L (RMAP)
      {;; For each map via a context-sensitive grammar
          rule, return a map for each way MG matches the
          left-hand-side of the rule.}
      (MAPCAR (F:L (LMAP) (SPLICE-MAPS LMAP RMAP))
        (MATCH-ONTO MG (CADR RMAP) FLAGS MG-CLEAN NIL)))
    (MAPCONC
      (F:L (RULE)
        {;; Return a map for each way the right-hand-side
            of a context-sensitive grammar rule matched MS.}
        (MAPCAR
          (F:L (TMAP) (LIST '--> (CAR RULE) TMAP))
          (MATCH-ONTO (CDR RULE) MS (CONS 'NO-CS-DERS FLAGS)
            NIL MS-CLEAN)))
      (CADDDR \CDL))))


(DE MATCH-INTO (MG MS FLAGS MG-CLEAN MS-CLEAN)
  {;; Return the MS consed onto a list of maps in which MG
      mapped into (not onto) MS. The code is simplified by
      assuming the first element in the list contains no
      submap. So, the original caller of this function should
      use the CDR of what is returned.}
  (AND MS
    (WITH [(MAPS
            (COND
              [(ATOM MS-CLEAN)
               {;; Atom not decomposable}
               (NCONS MS)]
              [T
               (WITH [(TCAR
                       (CONS (CAR MS-CLEAN)
                         (MATCH* MG (CAR MS-CLEAN)
                           FLAGS MG-CLEAN NIL)))
                      (TCDR
                       (CONS (CDR MS-CLEAN)
                         (MATCH* MG (CDR MS-CLEAN)
                           FLAGS MG-CLEAN NIL)))]
                 {;; If TCDR then two lists to join are
                     (old1 a b c) and (old2 x y z). Join old1
                     to everything in the second list, and
                     join everything in first list (except
```

```
                        old1) to old2. If TCDR is NIL then join
                        everything in first list to NIL.}
                   (COND
                     [TCDR
                      (NCONC
                        (MAPCAR
                          (F:L (TCDR*)
                            (CONS (CAR TCAR) TCDR*))
                          TCDR)
                        (MAPCAR
                          (F:L (TCAR*)
                            (CONS TCAR* (CAR TCDR)))
                          (CDR TCAR)))]
                     [T (MAPCAR (FUNCTION NCONS) TCAR)])))])))]
       (COND
         [(ATOM MS) MAPS]
         [(EQ (CAR MS) 'TAG)
          (MAPCAR (F:L (MAP) (CONS 'TAG MAP)) MAPS)]
         [T MAPS]))))

(DE MATCH-LIST-ONTO (MG MS FLAGS MG-CLEAN MS-CLEAN)
   {;; Return list of maps showing how decomposed MG maps
      onto decomposed MS as per FLAGS.}
   (WITH [TEMP]
     (AND
       (EVERY (F:L (MG* MS*)
           (WITH [(TMAPS (MATCH-ONTO MG* MS* FLAGS NIL NIL))]
             (AND TMAPS (PUSH TEMP TMAPS))))
         MG-CLEAN
         MS-CLEAN)
       (MAPCAR
         (F:L (MAPSET) (LIST '==> MG MS MAPSET))
         (ALL-COMBINATIONS (DREVERSE TEMP))))))

(DE MATCH-ONTO (MG MS FLAGS MG-CLEAN MS-CLEAN)
   {;; Return list of maps showing how MG maps onto MS as
      per FLAGS.}
   (AND MG MS
     (OR MG-CLEAN (SETQ MG-CLEAN (UNTAG-TRIM MG)))
     (OR MS-CLEAN (SETQ MS-CLEAN (UNTAG-TRIM MS)))
     (COND
       [(ATOM MG-CLEAN)
        (COND
          [(EQ MG-CLEAN MS-CLEAN)
```

```
                (NCONS (LIST '--> MG MS))]
        [T
         (WITH [(MAPS
                  (MATCH-ATOM-ONTO MG MS FLAGS
                    MG-CLEAN MS-CLEAN))]
            (COND
              [MAPS
               (COND
                 [(OR (MEMQ 'NO-AMB-DERS FLAGS)
                      (AND (NOT (ATOM MG))
                        (EQ (CAR MG) 'TAG)
                        (MEMQ 'NO-AMB-DERS-BELOW-TAG
                          FLAGS)))
                  (RPLACD MAPS NIL)
                  MAPS]
                 [(MEMQ 'NO-CS-DERS FLAGS)          MAPS]
                 [T
                  (NCONC MAPS
                    (MATCH-CS-ONTO MG MS FLAGS
                      MG-CLEAN MS-CLEAN))])]
              [(MEMQ 'NO-CS-DERS FLAGS)          NIL]
              [(SETQ MAPS
                 (MATCH-CS-ONTO MG MS FLAGS
                   MG-CLEAN MS-CLEAN))
               (COND
                 [(OR (MEMQ 'NO-AMB-DERS FLAGS)
                      (AND (NOT (ATOM MG))
                        (EQ (CAR MG) 'TAG)
                        (MEMQ 'NO-AMB-DERS-BELOW-TAG
                          FLAGS)))
                  (RPLACD MAPS NIL)
                  MAPS]
                 [T MAPS])])))])]
    [(ATOM MS-CLEAN)
     (COND
       [(MEMQ 'NO-CS-DERS FLAGS)          NIL]
       [T
        (WITH [(MAPS
                 (MATCH-CS-ONTO MG MS FLAGS
                   MG-CLEAN MS-CLEAN))]
           (AND MAPS
             (COND
               [(OR (MEMQ 'NO-AMB-DERS FLAGS)
                    (AND (NOT (ATOM MG))
```

```
                    (EQ (CAR MG) 'TAG)
                    (MEMQ 'NO-AMB-DERS-BELOW-TAG
                       FLAGS)))
                 (RPLACD MAPS NIL)
                 MAPS]
                [T MAPS])))])]
   [(EQUAL (LENGTH MG-CLEAN) (LENGTH MS-CLEAN))
    (WITH [(MAPS
              (MATCH-LIST-ONTO MG MS FLAGS
                 MG-CLEAN MS-CLEAN))]
       (COND
         [MAPS
          (COND
            [(OR (MEMQ 'NO-AMB-DERS FLAGS)
                 (AND (NOT (ATOM MG))
                    (EQ (CAR MG) 'TAG)
                    (MEMQ 'NO-AMB-DERS-BELOW-TAG
                       FLAGS)))
             (RPLACD MAPS NIL)
             MAPS]
            [(MEMQ 'NO-CS-DERS FLAGS)        MAPS]
            [T
             (NCONC MAPS
                (MATCH-CS-ONTO MG MS FLAGS
                   MG-CLEAN MS-CLEAN))])]
         [(MEMQ 'NO-CS-DERS FLAGS)        NIL]
         [(SETQ MAPS
             (MATCH-CS-ONTO MG MS FLAGS
                MG-CLEAN MS-CLEAN))
          (COND
            [(OR (MEMQ 'NO-AMB-DERS FLAGS)
                 (AND (NOT (ATOM MG))
                    (EQ (CAR MG) 'TAG)
                    (MEMQ
                       'NO-AMB-DERS-BELOW-TAG
                       FLAGS)))
             (RPLACD MAPS NIL)
             MAPS]
            [T MAPS])])]))))
```

A.5   Operators

These are the LEX operators. All have a LHS, RHS, and COMMENT property. Those that need to compute bindings also have a FORWARD

property. Those that need to compute bindings for a preimage also have a
BACKWARD property.

```
(DE AFFR-IZE (PAT)
  (PROG (MAPS BINDINGS E1 E2 ARG)
    {;; PAT - a single PAT, that does not contain an ffr.}
    {;; VALUE - a list containing the input PAT rewritten
       if necessary to be of the form of an a:ffr}
    (RETURN
     (COND
       [(MATCH 'A:FFR PAT '(NO-INTO-MAPS))
        {;; it is already in the desired form.}
        PAT]
       [(SETQ MAPS
          (MATCH '(&&OP IEXPR1 IEXPR2) PAT
            '(NO-AMB-DERS NO-INTO-MAPS)))
        (SETQ BINDINGS (FIND-BINDINGS (CAR MAPS)))
        (SETQ E1
          (AFFR-IZE (CDR (ASSOC 'IEXPR1 BINDINGS))))
        (SETQ E2
          (AFFR-IZE (CDR (ASSOC 'IEXPR2 BINDINGS))))
        (OR (EQUAL (SETQ ARG (ARG-IRE E1)) (ARG-IRE E2))
          (AND (MATCH (ARG-IRE E1)
                  (ARG-IRE E2) '(NO-INTO-MAPS))
            (SETQ ARG (ARG-IRE E2)))
          (AND (MATCH (ARG-IRE E2)
                  (ARG-IRE E1) '(NO-INTO-MAPS))
            (SETQ ARG (ARG-IRE E1)))
          (HELPME
            "PAT1 and PAT2 in AFFR-IZE do not"
            "have compatible arguments!"))
        (LIST
          (LIST
            (CDR (ASSOC '&&OP BINDINGS))
            (FN-IRE E1)
            (FN-IRE E2))
          ARG)]
       [(SETQ BINDINGS
          (FIND-BINDINGS
           (CAR
            (MATCH 'C PAT '(NO-AMB-DERS NO-INTO-MAPS)))))
        {;; This is a slightly different case from the
           others: you need to return some a:ffr, but with
```

```
                  what argument? Note the argument will be checked
                  later for being consistent with the argument of
                  the other expression if this is embedded in some
                  large expression. Therefore, we use the atom A:FR
                  which will consistent with any other legal
                  argument.}
            (SUBLIS BINDINGS '(C A:FR2))]
         [(SETQ BINDINGS
            (FIND-BINDINGS
             (CAR
              (MATCH 'A:FR2 PAT
                '(NO-AMB-DERS NO-INTO-MAPS)))))
           (SUBLIS BINDINGS '(ID A:FR2))]
         [T
          (HELPME
            "The expression passed to AFFR-IZE does not"
            "match any known descendant of PAT.")]))))

(DE ALG-EQUAL (P1 P2)
  (EQUAL (TRIM-ALL-TRAILING-DIGITS P1)
         (TRIM-ALL-TRAILING-DIGITS P2)))

(DE APPLY-OP (LHS-MAP RBPROG RHS-FORM)
  (WITH [(LB (FIND-BINDINGS LHS-MAP))]
    (WITH [(RB (EVAL RBPROG))]
      (COND
        [(EQ RB 'APPLY-OP-FAILS)
         {;; If it was not possible to compute the
             bindings needed to create the new RHS, then
             'APPLY-OP-FAILS is returned. So pass that along
             to caller.}
          RB]
        [T (REWRITE-MAP LHS-MAP LB RB RHS-FORM)]))))

(DE BOUND-VALUE (PAT BINDINGS)
  (OR (CDR (ASSOC PAT BINDINGS))
    (MSG 0 PAT " not found in bindings list." T)
    (HELPME)))

(DE CLEARESTIMATES (OPLIST)
  (MAPC
    (FUNCTION
     (LAMBDA (OP)
       (PUT OP NIL 'ESTIMATED-EXPANSION-COST)))
```

```
       (COND
         [(NULL OPLIST) \OPERATORS]
         [(ATOM OPLIST) (LIST OPLIST)]
         [T OPLIST]))
     T)

  (DE FIND-FRS (X)
    (COND
      [(NULL X) NIL]
      [(ATOM X)
       (COND
         [(MATCH 'C X '(NO-INTO-MAPS))                    NIL]
         [T (NCONS X)])]
      [T (NCONC (FIND-FRS (CADR X)) (FIND-FRS (CADDR X)))]))

  (DE MY*DIF (V1 V2)
    (COND
      [(AND (NUMBERP V1) (NUMBERP V2)) (*DIF V1 V2)]
      [T (LIST '- V1 V2)]))

  (DE MY*QUO (V1 V2)
    (COND
      [(AND (NUMBERP V1) (NUMBERP V2) (NOT (EQ V2 0)))
       (QUOTIENT V1 V2)]
      [T (LIST '\ V1 V2)]))

  (DE MY*TIMES (C1 C2) (RTIMES C1 C2))

  (DEFPROP OP1 (INT (SIN A:FR)) LHS)
  (DEFPROP OP1 ((* -1 COS) A:FR) RHS)
  (DEFPROP OP1 "INT sin(x)dx => -cos(x)" COMMENT)

  (DEFPROP OP10 (INT (COS A:FR)) LHS)
  (DEFPROP OP10 (SIN A:FR) RHS)
  (DEFPROP OP10 "INT cos(x) dx => sin(x)" COMMENT)

  (DEFPROP OP11 (INT ((+- FR1 FR2) A:FR)) LHS)
  (DEFPROP OP11 (+- (INT (FR1 A:FR)) (INT (FR2 A:FR))) RHS)
  (DEFPROP OP11
    "INT(f(x)+-g(x))dx => INT(f(x))dx+-INT(g(x))dx"
    COMMENT)

  (DEFPROP OP12 (INT1 ((*1 FR1 FR2) A:FR1)) LHS)
  (DEFPROP OP12
```

```
    (- (((*1 FR1 FR3) A:FR1) (INT1 ((*1 FR3 FR4) A:FR1)))
  RHS)
(DEFPROP OP12 "INTudv => uv-INTvdu, U=fr1,dV=fr2dx" COMMENT)
(DEFPROP OP12
  (PROG (DERIV-OF-FR1 INT-OF-FR2 LOCAL-STACK)
    {;; Important that we use INT1 instead of INT, *1
        instead of *, and A:FR1 instead of A:FR because these
        will be bound in a lambda expression. Without the
        trailing digits, they would conflict make unavailable
        the grammar nodes by the same name, thus not getting
        expected matches from MATCH. This is an issue here
        because of the recursive call to SOLVER.}
    (SETQ DERIV-OF-FR1
      (DERIVATIVE-FR (BOUND-VALUE 'FR1 LB)))
    (SETQ INT-OF-FR2
      (WITH [(RESOURCE-ALLOC
              (COND
                [\TREE-E-LIMITS
                  {;; Allocate ...}
                  (LIST
                    (*
                      0.333333
                      (- \TREE-E-TIME-LIMIT \TREE-E-TIME))
                    (*
                      0.333333
                      (-
                        \TREE-E-SPACE-LIMIT
                        \TREE-E-SPACE)))])
              SOLUTION]
            (PUSH LOCAL-STACK \NODELIST)
            (PUSH LOCAL-STACK \ALL-NODE-MOVES)
            (PUSH LOCAL-STACK \GOALNODENUMBER)
            (PUSH LOCAL-STACK \PRINTTHRESH)
            (PUSH LOCAL-STACK \TREE-E-LIMITS)
            (PUSH LOCAL-STACK \TREE-E-TIME-LIMIT)
            (PUSH LOCAL-STACK \TREE-E-TIME)
            (PUSH LOCAL-STACK \TREE-E-SPACE-LIMIT)
            (PUSH LOCAL-STACK \TREE-E-SPACE)
            (SETQ \PRINTTHRESH 1)
            (MSG 0 T (T (*PLUS \COLNUMBER 2))
              "OP12 calling SOLVER recursively." T)
            (SETQ SOLUTION
              (SOLVER
```

```
                  (LIST (BOUND-VALUE 'INT1 LB)
                    (LIST (BOUND-VALUE 'FR2 LB)
                      (BOUND-VALUE 'A:FR1 LB)))
                  RESOURCE-ALLOC))
              (SETQ \TREE-E-SPACE (POP LOCAL-STACK))
              (SETQ \TREE-E-SPACE-LIMIT (POP LOCAL-STACK))
              (SETQ \TREE-E-TIME (POP LOCAL-STACK))
              (SETQ \TREE-E-TIME-LIMIT (POP LOCAL-STACK))
              (SETQ \TREE-E-LIMITS (POP LOCAL-STACK))
              (SETQ \PRINTTHRESH (POP LOCAL-STACK))
              (COND
                [SOLUTION
                 (SETQ SOLUTION
                   (CADR (ASSOC \GOALNODENUMBER \NODELIST)))])
              (SETQ \GOALNODENUMBER (POP LOCAL-STACK))
              (SETQ \ALL-NODE-MOVES (POP LOCAL-STACK))
              (SETQ \NODELIST (POP LOCAL-STACK))
              SOLUTION))
          (RETURN
           (LIST
             (CONS 'FR3
               (COND
                 [INT-OF-FR2
                  (WITH [(TEMP (AFFR-IZE INT-OF-FR2))]
                    (COND
                      [(EQUAL (ARG-IRE TEMP)
                         (BOUND-VALUE 'A:FR1 LB))
                       (FN-IRE TEMP)]
                      [T (HELPME
                        {;; could be trouble - arg to int-of-fr2
                            is not the same as a:fr as bound in
                            left-hand-side of op12})])))]
                 [T {;; Integral of dv was not found.}
                    'FAIL]))
             (CONS 'FR4 DERIV-OF-FR1))))
      FORWARD)

(DEFPROP OP12
  (PROGN
    {;; Not yet written, so insure no funniness}
    'APPLY-OP-FAILS)
  BACKWARD)

(DEFPROP OP13 (INT ((* FR1 FR2) A:FR)) LHS)
```

```
(DEFPROP OP13
  (LIST (LIST '\ (LIST '^ FR1 2) 2) A:FR)
  RHS)
(DEFPROP OP13 "Int u*u'du => (u^2)/2" COMMENT)

(DEFPROP OP14 (INT (CPRIM A:FR)) LHS)
(DEFPROP OP14 ((* CPRIM ID) A:FR) RHS)
(DEFPROP OP14 "INT r dx => rx" COMMENT)

(DEFPROP OP15 (* O FR) LHS)
(DEFPROP OP15 O RHS)
(DEFPROP OP15 "O*fr => O" COMMENT)

(DEFPROP OP16 (INT (ID A:FR)) LHS)
(DEFPROP OP16 ((\ (^ ID 2) 2) A:FR) RHS)
(DEFPROP OP16 "INT x dx => (x^2)/2" COMMENT)

(DEFPROP OP17 (+ O FR) LHS)
(DEFPROP OP17 FR RHS)
(DEFPROP OP17 "O+fr => fr" COMMENT)

(DEFPROP OP18 (- FR O) LHS)
(DEFPROP OP18 FR RHS)
(DEFPROP OP18 "fr - O => fr" COMMENT)

(DEFPROP OP19 (^ FR1 FR2) LHS)
(DEFPROP OP19 (^ E (* FR2 (~ LN FR1))) RHS)
(DEFPROP OP19 "f(x)^g(x) => e^(g(x)ln(f(x)))" COMMENT)

(DEFPROP OP2 (INT ((^ ID CNM) A:FR)) LHS)
(DEFPROP OP2 ((\ (^ ID CNZ1) CNZ2) A:FR) RHS)
(DEFPROP OP2 "INT x^cnm dx => x^(cnm+1) / (cnm+1)" COMMENT)
(DEFPROP OP2
  (WITH [(TEMP (RADD1 (BOUND-VALUE 'CNM LB)))]
    (LIST (CONS 'CNZ1 TEMP) (CONS 'CNZ2 TEMP)))
  FORWARD)

(DEFPROP OP2
  (WITH [(TEMP1 (BOUND-VALUE 'CNZ1 LB))
         (TEMP2 (BOUND-VALUE 'CNZ2 LB))]
    (COND
      [(ALG-EQUAL TEMP1 TEMP2)
       (WITH [TEMP]
         (COND
```

```
              [(ATOM (SETQ TEMP (RSUB1 TEMP1)))
               (NCONS (CONS 'CNM TEMP))]
              [(SETQ
                 TEMP
                 (LOOKUP-OR-MAKE
                   TEMP1
                   '(RADD1 LVAR)
                   'CNZ))
               (NCONS (CONS 'CNM TEMP))]
             [T 'APPLY-OP-FAILS]))]
        [T 'APPLY-OP-FAILS]))
  BACKWARD)

(DEFPROP OP20 (~ LN EXP) LHS)
(DEFPROP OP20 ID RHS)
(DEFPROP OP20 "ln(exp(x)) => x" COMMENT)

(DEFPROP OP21 (~ EXP LN) LHS)
(DEFPROP OP21 ID RHS)
(DEFPROP OP21 "exp(ln(x)) => x" COMMENT)

(DEFPROP OP22 (* C1 C2) LHS)
(DEFPROP OP22 C3 RHS)
(DEFPROP OP22 "c1*c2 => c3" COMMENT)
(DEFPROP OP22
  (NCONS
   (CONS C3
     (RTIMES
       (BOUND-VALUE 'C1 LB)
       (BOUND-VALUE 'C2 LB))))
  FORWARD)

(DEFPROP OP22
  (WITH [(TEMP (BOUND-VALUE 'C3 LB))]
    (LIST
      (CONS 'C1 (LIST '\ TEMP 'C988))
      (CONS 'C2 'C988)))
  BACKWARD)

(DEFPROP OP23 TAN LHS)
(DEFPROP OP23 (\ SIN COS) RHS)
(DEFPROP OP23 "tan(x) => sin(x)/cos(x)" COMMENT)

(DEFPROP OP24 COT LHS)
(DEFPROP OP24 (^ TAN -1) RHS)
(DEFPROP OP24 "cot(x) => 1/tan(x)" COMMENT)
```

```
(DEFPROP OP25 SEC LHS)
(DEFPROP OP25 (^ COS -1) RHS)
(DEFPROP OP25 "sec(x) => 1/cos(x)" COMMENT)

(DEFPROP OP26 CSC LHS)
(DEFPROP OP26 (^ SIN -1) RHS)
(DEFPROP OP26 "csc(x) => 1/sin(x)" COMMENT)

(DEFPROP OP27 (^ SIN 2) LHS)
(DEFPROP OP27 (- 1 (^ COS 2)) RHS)
(DEFPROP OP27 "sin^2(x) => 1-cos^2(x)" COMMENT)

(DEFPROP OP28 (* 0 IEXPR) LHS)
(DEFPROP OP28 0 RHS)
(DEFPROP OP28 "0 * IEXPR => 0" COMMENT)

(DEFPROP OP29 (* 1 IEXPR) LHS)
(DEFPROP OP29 IEXPR RHS)
(DEFPROP OP29 "1 * IEXPR => IEXPR" COMMENT)

(DEFPROP OP3 (INT ((* CPRIM FR) A:FR)) LHS)
(DEFPROP OP3 (* CPRIM (INT (FR A:FR))) RHS)
(DEFPROP OP3 "INTcf(x)dx => cINTf(x)dx" COMMENT)

(DEFPROP OP30 (- IEXPR 0) LHS)
(DEFPROP OP30 IEXPR RHS)
(DEFPROP OP30 "IEXPR - 0 => IEXPR" COMMENT)

(DEFPROP OP31 (\ FR1 FR2) LHS)
(DEFPROP OP31 (* FR1 (^ FR2 -1)) RHS)
(DEFPROP OP31 "fr1/fr2 => fr1*(fr2^-1)" COMMENT)

(DEFPROP OP32 (^ SIN 2) LHS)
(DEFPROP OP32 (\ (- 1 (~ COS (* 2 ID))) 2) RHS)
(DEFPROP OP32 "sin^2(x) => (1-cos(2x))/2" COMMENT)

(DEFPROP OP33 (+* FR1 (+* FR2 FR3)) LHS)
(DEFPROP OP33 (+* FR2 (+* FR1 FR3)) RHS)
(DEFPROP OP33
  "(+* fr1 (+* fr2 fr3)) => (+* fr2 (+* fr1 fr3))"
  COMMENT)

(DEFPROP OP34 (^ COS 2) LHS)
(DEFPROP OP34 (\ (+ 1 (~ COS (* 2 ID))) 2) RHS)
(DEFPROP OP34 "cos^2(x) => (1+cos(2x))/2" COMMENT)
```

```
(DEFPROP OP35 (+* FR1 (+- FR2 FR3)) LHS)
(DEFPROP OP35 (+- (+* FR1 FR2) (+* FR1 FR3)) RHS)
(DEFPROP OP35 "f1+*(f2+-f3) => (f1+*f2)+-(f1+*f3)" COMMENT)

(DEFPROP OP35
  (PROGN {;; for now} 'APPLY-OP-FAILS)
  BACKWARD)

(DEFPROP OP36 (+ C1 C2) LHS)
(DEFPROP OP36 C3 RHS)
(DEFPROP OP36 "(+ r1 r2) => evaluated (r1 + r2)" COMMENT)
(DEFPROP OP36
  (NCONS
   (CONS C3
     (RPLUS
       (BOUND-VALUE 'C1 LB)
       (BOUND-VALUE 'C2 LB))))
  FORWARD)

(DEFPROP OP36
  (PROGN
    {;; Eventually write as (+ (- c3 c5) c5) where c5 is
        unique, but now just prevent funniness}
    'APPLY-OP-FAILS)
  BACKWARD)

(DEFPROP OP37 (INT ((* FR1 FR2) A:FR)) LHS)
(DEFPROP OP37
  (PROG (S1 S2 CONSTANT)
    (SETQ S1 (DERIVATIVE-FR FR1))
    (SETQ S2 (SIMPLIFY-FR FR2))
    {;; See whether they are equal to within a constant.}
    (SETQ CONSTANT
      (OR
        (CAR
         (MATCH (NCONS (LIST '* 'R S1)) (NCONS S2)))
        (CAR
         (MATCH (NCONS (LIST '* 'R S2)) (NCONS S1)))))
    {;; If so, then introduce the constant.}
    (COND
      [CONSTANT
       (SETQ CONSTANT
         (CDR (ASSOC 'R (FIND-BINDINGS CONSTANT))))
       (RETURN
```

```
        (LIST INT
          (LIST
            (LIST '\
              (LIST '*
                CONSTANT
                (LIST '* FR1 FR2))
              CONSTANT)
            A:FR)))])
    (RETURN 'FAIL))
  RHS)
(DEFPROP OP37
  "INT r? * u * u' du => INT r * u * u' du"
  COMMENT)


(DEFPROP OP37 (PROGN 'APPLY-OP-FAILS) BACKWARD)


(DEFPROP OP38 (* (^ FR1 FR2) (^ FR3 FR4)) LHS)
(DEFPROP OP38 (LIST ^ FR1 (LIST '+ FR2 FR4)) RHS)
(DEFPROP OP38
  "(* (^ fr1 fr2)(^ fr1 fr3)) => (^ fr1 (+ fr2 fr3))"
  COMMENT)


(DEFPROP OP39 (* FR1 (^ FR2 FR3)) LHS)
(DEFPROP OP39 (LIST ^ FR1 (LIST '+ FR3 1)) RHS)
(DEFPROP OP39
  "(* fr1 (^ fr1 fr2)) => (^ fr1 (+ fr2 1))"
  COMMENT)


(DEFPROP OP4 (INT ((^ ID -1) A:FR)) LHS)
(DEFPROP OP4 (LN A:FR) RHS)
(DEFPROP OP4 "INT x^(-1) dx => ln(x)" COMMENT)


(DEFPROP OP40 (^ FR 0) LHS)
(DEFPROP OP40 1 RHS)
(DEFPROP OP40 "(^ fr 0) => 1" COMMENT)


(DEFPROP OP41 (* FR1 FR2) LHS)
(DEFPROP OP41 (LIST '^ FR1 2) RHS)
(DEFPROP OP41 "fr1 * fr1 => (^ fr1 2)" COMMENT)


(DEFPROP OP42 (+* FR1 FR2) LHS)
(DEFPROP OP42 (+* FR2 FR1) RHS)
(DEFPROP OP42 "f(x)*g(x) => g(x)*f(x)" COMMENT)
```

```
(DEFPROP OP43 (INT ((* (~ FR1 FR2) FR3) A:FR)) LHS)
(DEFPROP OP43 (INT (FR4 A:FR2)) RHS)
(DEFPROP OP43 "INT f(g(x))g'(x)dx => INT f(u)du" COMMENT)
(DEFPROP OP43
  (WITH [(DER
            (DERIVATIVE-FR
             (TRIM-ALL-TRAILING-DIGITS
              (BOUND-VALUE 'FR2 LB))))]
    (COND
      [(ALG-EQUAL DER (BOUND-VALUE 'FR3 LB))
       (LIST
         (CONS 'FR4 (BOUND-VALUE 'FR1 LB))
         (CONS 'A:FR2 'U99))]
      [T
       (LIST
         (CONS 'FR4 'FAIL)
         (CONS 'A:FR2 'FAIL))]))
  FORWARD)

(DEFPROP OP43
  (WITH [(TEMP (BOUND-VALUE 'FR4 LB))]
    {;; This isn't right because it does not impose
       constraint that FR3 be the derivative of FR2. Am
       putting this here now to let the rest of the
       propagation step go through.}
    (LIST (CONS 'FR1 TEMP)))
  BACKWARD)

(DEFPROP OP46 (INT ((* (^ FR1 R) FR2) A:FR)) LHS)
(DEFPROP OP46
  (LIST 'INT (LIST (LIST ^ 'ID R) A:FR))
  RHS)
(DEFPROP OP46
  "INT (f(x)^r)*f'(x) dx => INT v^r dv (substitute v for f(x))"
  COMMENT)

(DEFPROP OP47 INT LHS)
(DEFPROP OP47
  (LIST (LIST '~ '(~ LN ABS) FR1) A:FR)
  RHS)
(DEFPROP OP47 "Int u'*(u^-1) du => ln(abs(u))" COMMENT)

(DEFPROP OP48 (\ FR1 FR2) LHS)
(DEFPROP OP48 (* -1 (\ (* -1 FR1) FR2)) RHS)
(DEFPROP OP48 "fr1/fr2 => -(-fr1/fr2)" COMMENT)
```

```
(DEFPROP OP49 (INT (TAN A:FR)) LHS)
(DEFPROP OP49 ((~ LN (~ ABS COS)) A:FR) RHS)
(DEFPROP OP49 "Int tan(x) dx => ln(abs(cos(x)))" COMMENT)

(DEFPROP OP5 (INT (EXP A:FR)) LHS)
(DEFPROP OP5 (EXP A:FR) RHS)
(DEFPROP OP5 "INT exp dx => exp" COMMENT)

(DEFPROP OP50 (^ FR1 C2) LHS)
(DEFPROP OP50 (^ (^ FR1 2) C3) RHS)
(DEFPROP OP50 "f1^f2 => (f1^2)^(f2/2)" COMMENT)
(DEFPROP OP50
  (WITH [AB]
    (SETQ AB
      (LIST
        (CONS 'C3
          (MY*QUO (BOUND-VALUE 'C2 LB) 2.0))))
    AB)
  FORWARD)

(DEFPROP OP50
  (WITH [TEMP]
    (COND
      [(ATOM
        (SETQ TEMP
          (MY*TIMES 2.0 (BOUND-VALUE 'C3 LB))))
       {;; If were able to do the multiplication, then
           fine.}
       (NCONS (CONS 'C2 TEMP))]
      [(SETQ TEMP
        (LOOKUP-OR-MAKE
          (BOUND-VALUE 'C3 LB)
          '(MY*QUO LVAR 2.0)
          'C))
       {;; Otherwise, if able to back-propagate the set,
           then use that.}
       (NCONS (CONS 'C2 TEMP))]
      [T {;; Otherwise, signal failure.}
        'APPLY-OP-FAILS]))
  BACKWARD)

(DEFPROP OP51 (^ FR3 C2) LHS)
(DEFPROP OP51 (* (^ FR1 C1) FR2) RHS)
(DEFPROP OP51 "f(x)^r => f(x)^(r-1) * f(x)" COMMENT)
```

```
(DEFPROP OP51
  (WITH [(TEMP1 (RSUB1 (BOUND-VALUE 'C2 LB)))
         (TEMP2 (BOUND-VALUE 'FR3 LB))]
    (LIST
      (CONS 'C1 TEMP1)
      (CONS 'FR1 TEMP2)
      (CONS 'FR2 TEMP2)))
  FORWARD)

(DEFPROP OP51
  (WITH [(TEMP1 (BOUND-VALUE 'FR1 LB))
         (TEMP2 (BOUND-VALUE 'FR2 LB))
         TEMP]
    (COND
      [(ALG-EQUAL TEMP1 TEMP2)
       (COND
         [(NUMBERP (BOUND-VALUE 'C1 LB))
          (LIST (CONS 'FR3 TEMP1)
            (CONS 'C2
              (ADD1 (BOUND-VALUE 'C1 LB))))]
         [(SETQ  TEMP
            (LOOKUP-OR-MAKE
              (BOUND-VALUE 'C1 LB)
              '(RADD1 LVAR)
              'C))
          (LIST
            (CONS 'C2 TEMP)
            (CONS 'FR3 TEMP1))]
         [T 'APPLY-OP-FAILS])]
      [T 'APPLY-OP-FAILS]))
  BACKWARD)

(DEFPROP OP52 (^ COS 2) LHS)
(DEFPROP OP52 (- 1 (^ SIN 2)) RHS)
(DEFPROP OP52 "cos^2(x) => 1-sin^2(x)" COMMENT)

(DEFPROP OP53 (~ POLY FR) LHS)
(DEFPROP OP53 (SUBST FR 'ID POLY) RHS)
(DEFPROP OP53
  "poly(f1(x)) => f2(x) replacing id with f1 in poly"
  COMMENT)

(DEFPROP OP54 (INT ((* (^ (~ POLY FR1) C) FR2) A:FR)) LHS)
(DEFPROP OP54 (LIST INT (LIST (LIST ^ POLY C) A:FR)) RHS)
```

```
(DEFPROP OP54
  "Int poly(f(x))^r * f'(x)dx => Int poly(u)^r du"
  COMMENT)

(DEFPROP OP6 (^ E FR) LHS)
(DEFPROP OP6 (~ EXP FR) RHS)
(DEFPROP OP6 "e^f(x) => exp(f(x))" COMMENT)

(DEFPROP OP7 (INT (LN A:FR)) LHS)
(DEFPROP OP7 ((- (* ID LN) ID) A:FR) RHS)
(DEFPROP OP7 "INT ln(x) dx => x ln(x) - x" COMMENT)

(DEFPROP OP8 (* 1 FR) LHS)
(DEFPROP OP8 FR RHS)
(DEFPROP OP8 "1*fr => fr" COMMENT)

(DEFPROP OP9 FR LHS)
(DEFPROP OP9 (~ POLY FR2) RHS)
(DEFPROP OP9 "rewrite fr1 as poly(fr2) if possible" COMMENT)
(DEFPROP OP9
  (WITH [(TEMP1
           (TRIM-ALL-TRAILING-DIGITS
             (BOUND-VALUE 'FR LB)))
         TEMP2]
    (COND
      [(EQ
         (LENGTH (SETQ TEMP2 (UNION (FIND-FRS TEMP1) NIL)))
         1)
       (LIST (CONS 'POLY (SUBST-ID TEMP1))
         (CONS 'FR2 (CAR TEMP2)))]
      [(ZEROP (LENGTH TEMP2))
       (LIST (CONS 'POLY 'ID)
         (CONS 'FR2 (BOUND-VALUE 'FR LB)))]
      [T (LIST (CONS 'POLY 'FAIL)
             (CONS 'FR2 'FAIL))]))
  FORWARD)

(DEFPROP OP9
  (WITH [(TEMP
           (SUBST
             (BOUND-VALUE 'FR2 LB)
             'ID
             (TRIM-ALL-TRAILING-DIGITS
               (BOUND-VALUE 'POLY LB))))]
    (NCONS (CONS 'FR TEMP)))
  BACKWARD)
```

```
(DE RADD1 (EXP)
  {;; VALUE - if exp is a number then the value of exp+1;
      else an algebraic EXPRession in which 1. has been added
      to exp}
  (COND
    [(NUMBERP EXP) (ADD1 EXP)]
    [T (LIST '+ EXP 1)]))

(DE REWRITE-MAP (LHS-MAP LB RB RHS-FORM)
  (COND
    [(ATOM LHS-MAP) LHS-MAP]
    [(MEMQ (CAR LHS-MAP) '(--> ==>))
     (REWRITE-MAP* (APPEND LB RB) RHS-FORM)]
    [T (MAPCAR
         (F:L (MAP*) (REWRITE-MAP MAP* LB RB RHS-FORM))
         LHS-MAP)]))

(DE REWRITE-MAP* (BINDINGS FORM)
  (COND
    [(ATOM FORM)
     (WITH [(TEMP (ASSOC FORM BINDINGS))]
       {;; By using ASSOC we assume that bindings are
           always to atoms. That is a limitation we allow
           here, but the grammar and FIND-BINDINGS and MATCH
           are more general than this. They do permit
           context-sensitive rules.}
       (COND [TEMP (CDR TEMP)]
             [T FORM]))]
    [T (MAPCAR
         (F:L (FORM*) (REWRITE-MAP* BINDINGS FORM*))
         FORM)]))

(DE RPLUS (RN1 RN2)
  (COND
    [(AND (NUMBERP RN1) (NUMBERP RN2)) (+ RN1 RN2)]
    [T (LIST '+ RN1 RN2)]))

(DE RSUB1 (EXP)
  (COND
    [(NUMBERP EXP) (SUB1 EXP)]
    [T (LIST '- EXP 1)]))

(DE RTIMES (RN1 RN2)
  (COND
    [(AND (NUMBERP RN1) (NUMBERP RN2)) (* RN1 RN2)]
    [T (LIST '* RN1 RN2)]))
```

```
(DE SUBST-ID (X)
  (COND
    [(NULL X) NIL]
    [(ATOM X)
     (COND
       [(MATCH 'C X '(NO-INTO-MAPS))          X]
       [T 'ID])]
    [T (CONS (CAR X) (MAPCAR (FUNCTION SUBST-ID) (CDR X)))]))

(DE UNIQUE-OPNAME (OPNAME)
  (COND
    [(MEMQ OPNAME OPERATORSFNS)
     (WITH [(DIGIT (READLIST (CDDR (AEXPLODEC OPNAME))))]
       (UNIQUE-OPNAME
        (READLIST
         (CONS 'O
           (CONS 'P (AEXPLODEC (ADD1 DIGIT)))))))]
    [T OPNAME]))

(DV \DISABLED-OPERATORS (OP13 OP28 OP29 OP30 OP36
       OP37 OP38 OP39 OP41 OP46 OP47 OP53 OP54))

(DV \OPERATORS (OP1 OP2 OP3 OP4 OP5 OP6 OP7 OP8 OP10
       OP11 OP12 OP14 OP15 OP16 OP17 OP18 OP19 OP22
       OP23 OP24 OP25 OP26 OP27 OP31 OP32 OP33 OP34
       OP35 OP40 OP42 OP43 OP48 OP49 OP50 OP51 OP52 OP9))
```

A.6　Utilities

This section contains miscellaneous utilities from LEX that are used by STABB.

```
(DE ALL-COMBINATIONS (LST)
  {;; Given a list of lists, returns all combinations of
     the top-level elements of the lists. Try
     (ALL-COMBINATIONS '((A B)(C D)(E))) as an example.}
  (PROG (TEMP)
    (RETURN
     (COND
       [(NULL LST) NIL]
       [(SETQ TEMP (ALL-COMBINATIONS (CDR LST)))
        (MAPCONC
          (F:L (EL)
            (MAPCAR (F:L (COMB) (CONS EL COMB)) TEMP))
          (CAR LST))]
       [T (MAPCAR (FUNCTION NCONS) (CAR LST))]))))
```

```
(DE ARG-IRE (IRE)
  {;; IRE - an implicit relational expression; see matcher
      documentation.}
  {;; VALUE - the arguments to this IRE - for now that's
      the cadar of the list.}
  (CADR IRE))

(DE BINDING-FITS-MAP-P (BINDING MAP)
  (SET-EQUALS BINDING (FIND-BINDINGS MAP)))

(DE COMPOSE-BINDINGS (B1 B2)
  {;; VALUE - the binding corresponding to the composition
      B2 applied to B1}
  (MAPCAR
    (F:L (PAIR) (CONS (CAR PAIR) (SUBLIS B2 (CDR PAIR))))
    B1))

(DE DERIVATIVE-FR (FRVAL)
  {;; DERIVATIVE-FR* is very general, and returns ugly,
      verbose, highly complicated expressions. It is useful to
      simplify that output.}
  (SIMPLIFY-FR (DERIVATIVE-FR* FRVAL)))

(DE DERIVATIVE-FR* (FRVAL)
  {;; Computes the derivative of a given 'fr.}
  {;; The 'fr is assumed to be legal (recognized as an 'fr
      by MATCH).}
  (PROG (SECOND)
    (RETURN
    (COND
      [(NUMBERP FRVAL) 0]
      [(EQ FRVAL 'ID)         1]
      [(EQ FRVAL 'SIN)        'COS]
      [(EQ FRVAL 'COS)        '(* -1 SIN)]
      [(EQ FRVAL 'TAN)        '(^ SEC 2)]
      [(EQ FRVAL 'CSC)        '(* -1 CSC COT)]
      [(EQ FRVAL 'SEC)        '(* SEC TAN)]
      [(EQ FRVAL 'COT)        '(* -1 (^ CSC 2))]
      [(EQ FRVAL 'LN)         '(^ ID -1)]
      [(EQ FRVAL 'EXP)        FRVAL]
      [(EQ FRVAL 'E)        FRVAL]
      [(EQ FRVAL 'ABS)        '(\ ABS ID)]
      [(EQ (CAR FRVAL) '+)
```

```
{;; Handles one or more operands.}
(CONS '+
  (MAPCAR
    (F:L (ITEM) (DERIVATIVE-FR* ITEM))
    (CDR FRVAL)))]
[(EQ (CAR FRVAL) '-)
 {;; Handles two operands.}
 (LIST '-
   (DERIVATIVE-FR* (CADR FRVAL))
   (DERIVATIVE-FR* (CADDR FRVAL)))]
[(EQ (CAR FRVAL) '*)
 {;; Handles two or more operands.}
 (LIST '+
   (LIST '*
     (CADR FRVAL)
     (DERIVATIVE-FR*
      (SETQ SECOND
        (COND
          [(GT 3 (LENGTH FRVAL))
           (CONS '* (CDDR FRVAL))]
          [T (CADDR FRVAL)]))))
   (LIST '*
     (DERIVATIVE-FR* (CADR FRVAL))
     SECOND))]
[(EQ (CAR FRVAL) '\)
 {;; Handles two operands.}
 (LIST '\
   (LIST '-
     (LIST '*
       (CADDR FRVAL)
       (DERIVATIVE-FR* (CADR FRVAL)))
     (LIST '*
       (DERIVATIVE-FR* (CADDR FRVAL))
       (CADR FRVAL)))
   (LIST '^ (CADDR FRVAL) 2))]
[(EQ (CAR FRVAL) '^)
 {;; Handles two operands.}
 (LIST '*
   (LIST '^ (CADR FRVAL) (CADDR FRVAL))
   (DERIVATIVE-FR*
    (LIST '*
      (CADDR FRVAL)
      (LIST '~ 'LN (CADR FRVAL)))))]
```

```
        [(EQ (CAR FRVAL) '~)
         {;; Handles two operands.}
         (LIST '*
           (LIST '~
             (DERIVATIVE-FR* (CADR FRVAL))
             (CADDR FRVAL))
           (DERIVATIVE-FR* (CADDR FRVAL)))]))))

(DE DISASSOCIATE-FR (COMB OLDARGS NEWARGS)
  (COND
    [(NULL NEWARGS) OLDARGS]
    [(OR (ATOM (CAR NEWARGS))
         (NOT (EQ (CAAR NEWARGS) COMB)))
     (DISASSOCIATE-FR COMB
       (CONS (CAR NEWARGS) OLDARGS)
       (CDR NEWARGS))]
    [T (DISASSOCIATE-FR COMB
         OLDARGS
         (APPEND (CDAR NEWARGS) (CDR NEWARGS)))]))

(DE FIND-BINDINGS (MAP)
  {;; Returns a list of pairs where each CAR is a portion
      of the MG, and the CDR is the portion of the MS which it
      matched.}
  (COND
    [(ATOM MAP) {;; Atom can't be a mapping.}        NIL]
    [(MEMQ (CAR MAP) '(--> ==>))
     {;; Have a map, now find out what top level of map
         binds to.}
     (FIND-BINDINGS* (CADR MAP) (CADDR MAP))]
    [T (MAPCONC (FUNCTION FIND-BINDINGS) MAP)]))

(DE FIND-BINDINGS* (MG MS)
  {;; Given an MG and the rest of the map to/via MS,
      return the binding of MG to corresponding part of MS. If
      MG is a list, this may call for some decomposition. In
      any case, a list of pairs (MG . MS) is returned.}
  (COND
    [(ATOM MS) (NCONS (CONS MG MS))]
    [(MEMQ (CAR MS) '(--> ==>))
     {;; Another map, try again.}
     (FIND-BINDINGS* MG (CADDR MS))]
    [(ATOM MG) (NCONS (CONS MG MS))]
    [(EQUAL (LENGTH MG) (LENGTH MS))
```

```
    {;; Assume there is a one to one correspondence.}
    (MAPCONC (FUNCTION FIND-BINDINGS*) MG MS)]
   [T (NCONS (CONS MG MS))])))

(DE FIND-MAP-EMBEDDINGS (ARGMAP)
  {;; ARGMAP is an ire-map, embedded or not.}
  {;; Returns list of pointers to embedded ire-map and
      every list in which the ire-map is embedded.}
  (PROG (TEMP)
    (RETURN
     (COND
       [(ATOM ARGMAP)
        {;; Atom is neither a map nor a list.}
        NIL]
       [(MEMQ (CAR ARGMAP) '(--> ==>))
        {;; Return list with pointer to embedded ire-map.}
        (NCONS ARGMAP)]
       [(SETQ TEMP
          (MAPCONC
            (FUNCTION FIND-MAP-EMBEDDINGS)
            ARGMAP))
        {;; Include pointer to list which embeds the
            ire-map.}
        (CONS ARGMAP TEMP)])))))

(DE FN-IRE (IRE)
  {;; IRE - an implicit relational expression; see matcher
      documentation}
  {;; VALUE - the function in the ire - for now that's the
      caar of the list}
  (CAR IRE))

(DE GEN-INSTS (OP1 STATE)
  (MAPCAR
    (F:L (MAP)
      (LIST 'NODE-NUM
        STATE
        (LIST OP1 MAP 'VAL1 'VAL2 'VAL3)))
    (MATCH (GET OP1 'LHS)
      STATE
      '(NO-AMB-DERS))))

(DE GENMAPS (MG-SD MS-SD FLAGS BINDING)
```

```
{;; takes same arguments as MATCH as well as an
    additional argument: BINDING}
{;; VALUE - a list of mappinglists of mg-sd to ms-sd
    that have BINDING as their binding}
(SUBSET
  (F:L (MAP) (SET-EQUALS BINDING (FIND-BINDINGS MAP)))
  (MATCH MG-SD MS-SD FLAGS)))

(DE INST-TO-HDESCR (INST)
  {;; Returns hdescr which corresponds to INST.}
  (LIST (CADR INST) (FIND-BINDINGS (CADR (CADDR INST)))))

(DE LEAST-HDESCRS (PLIS)
  {;; PLIS - a list of heuristic descriptions.}
  {;; VALUE - a list of the least specific heuristic
      descriptions from PLIS.}
  (PROG (TMPPLIS)
    (SETQ PLIS (REMOVE-DUPLICATES PLIS))
    (SETQ TMPPLIS (APPEND PLIS NIL))
    (MAPC
      (FUNCTION
        (LAMBDA (ZZG)
          (COND
            [(NOT
               (SOME
                 (FUNCTION
                   (LAMBDA (GT)
                     (AND
                       (NEQ GT ZZG)
                       (MORE-SPECIFIC-HEURISTIC ZZG GT))))
                 TMPPLIS))]
            [T (SETQ TMPPLIS (DREMOVE ZZG TMPPLIS))])))
      PLIS)
    (RETURN TMPPLIS)))

(DE LEASTPATTERNS (PLIS)
  {;; PLIS - a list of generalizations.}
  {;; VALUE - a list of the least specific generalizations
      from PLIS.}
  (PROG (TMPPLIS)
    (SETQ PLIS (REMOVE-DUPLICATES PLIS))
    (SETQ TMPPLIS (APPEND PLIS NIL))
    (MAPC
```

```
      (FUNCTION
       (LAMBDA (ZZG)
         (COND
           [(NOT
             (SOME
               (FUNCTION
                (LAMBDA (GT)
                  (AND (NEQ GT ZZG)
                    (MATCH GT ZZG '(NO-AMB-DERS)))))
               TMPPLIS))]
           [T (SETQ TMPPLIS (DREMOVE ZZG TMPPLIS))]))))
     PLIS)
    (RETURN TMPPLIS)))

(DE MAX-HDESCRS (PLIS)
  {;; VALUE - a list of the maximally specific heuristic
     descriptions from PLIS.}
  (PROG (TMPPLIS)
    (SETQ PLIS (REMOVE-DUPLICATES PLIS))
    (SETQ TMPPLIS (APPEND PLIS NIL))
    (MAPC
      (FUNCTION
       (LAMBDA (G)
         (COND
           [(SOME
               (FUNCTION
                (LAMBDA (GT)
                  (AND (NEQ GT G)
                    (MORE-SPECIFIC-HEURISTIC GT G))))
               TMPPLIS)
             (SETQ TMPPLIS (DREMOVE G TMPPLIS))])))
     PLIS)
    (RETURN TMPPLIS)))

(DE MAXPATTERNS (PLIS)
  {;; PLIS - a list of generalizations.}
  {;; VALUE - a list of the maximally specific
     generalizations from PLIS.}
  (PROG (TMPPLIS)
    (SETQ PLIS (REMOVE-DUPLICATES PLIS))
    (SETQ TMPPLIS (APPEND PLIS NIL))
    (MAPC
      (FUNCTION
       (LAMBDA (G)
```

```
            (COND
              [(SOME
                 (FUNCTION
                  (LAMBDA (GT)
                    (AND (NEQ GT G)
                         (MATCH G GT '(NO-AMB-DERS)))))
                  TMPPLIS)
                 (SETQ TMPPLIS (DREMOVE G TMPPLIS))]))))
         PLIS)
       (RETURN TMPPLIS)))

(DE PRIN-INST (INST PRIN-COLUMN PRIN-HEADER)
   {;; Prints an INST. Always returns NIL. PRIN-HEADER
      should be a string. Something like 'Apply' or 'Do not
      apply' or 'Avoid application of' or 'Do not avoid
      application of'.}
   (MSG O (T (OR PRIN-COLUMN (SETQ PRIN-COLUMN 1)))
     (C PRIN-HEADER) " " (CAADDR INST) " to state #"
     (CAR INST) (T (*PLUS 2 PRIN-COLUMN)) "State #"
     (CAR INST) ":"
     (E (SPRINT (CADR INST) (*PLUS 14 PRIN-COLUMN)))
     (T (*PLUS 2 PRIN-COLUMN)) "Bindings:"
     (E (SPRINT
          (FIND-BINDINGS (CADR (CADDR INST)))
          (*PLUS PRIN-COLUMN 14)))))

(DE PRINHDESCR (H PRIN-COL)
  {;; H - an hdescr}
  (OR PRIN-COL (SETQ PRIN-COL 1))
  (SPRINT (CAR H) PRIN-COL)
  (SPRINT (CADR H) (PLUS 2 PRIN-COL)))

(DE PRINHEURISTIC (HEUR PRIN-COL)
  {;; M - an S or G set of hdescrs}
  (OR PRIN-COL (SETQ PRIN-COL 1))
  (MAPC
    (F:L (M)
      (MSG (T PRIN-COL) (CAR M) (T (PLUS 3 PRIN-COL))
        (CADR M)
        (E
         (MAPC
           (F:L (P)
             (PRINHDESCR P (PLUS 6 PRIN-COL))
             (TERPRI))
```

```
          (CDDR M)))
       T))
   HEUR))

(DE PRINTVSS (HNAME EVIDENCE-FLAG)
  {;; For printing out concentric version spaces of HNAME.}
  {;; If EVIDENCE-FLAG = T also prints out list of
     training instances.}
  (MSG O T "----- Heuristic " HNAME
    " -----" T T (T 3)
    "If part of the state is of the form "
    HNAME T (T 5) "then "
    (C
     (COND
       [(EQ 'USE (GET HNAME 'RECOMMENDATION))
        "apply"]
       [(EQ 'AVOID
          (GET HNAME 'RECOMMENDATION))
        "do not apply"]
       [T "ponder strange heuristic for"]))
    " operator "
    (GET HNAME 'RECOMMENDED-OPERATOR)
    "." T T (T 3)
    (GET HNAME 'RECOMMENDED-OPERATOR)
    ": " (C
     (GET (GET HNAME 'RECOMMENDED-OPERATOR)
       'COMMENT))
    T T (T 3) "After "
    (E
     (COND
       [(EQ (LENGTH (GET HNAME 'EVIDENCE)) 1)
        (MSG "1 training instance")]
       [T
        (MSG
          (LENGTH (GET HNAME 'EVIDENCE))
          " training instances")]))
    ", version spaces for " HNAME
    " are:" T T)
  (COND
    [(OR
        (EQSTR \USER-NAME "Paul Utgoff")
        (EQSTR \USER-NAME "Ranan Banerji")
        (EQSTR \USER-NAME "Rich Keller"))
```

```
      (MSG (T 3) "Gs:")
      (PRINHEURISTIC (GET HNAME 'GS) 8)
      (MSG (T 3) "Ss:")
      (PRINHEURISTIC (REVERSE (GET HNAME 'SS)) 8)]
    [T
      (MSG (T 3) "Ss:")
      (PRINHEURISTIC (GET HNAME 'SS) 8)
      (MSG (T 3) "Gs:")
      (PRINHEURISTIC (REVERSE (GET HNAME 'GS)) 8)])
  (COND
    [EVIDENCE-FLAG
      (MSG O (T 3) "Evidence for " HNAME ":" T)
      (MAPC
        (F:L (INST)
          (PRIN-INST
            (CDR INST)
            6
            (COND
              [(EQ (CAR INST) 'POS)
               (COND
                 [(EQ (GET HNAME 'RECOMMENDATION)
                     'USE)
                  "Apply"]
                 [T "Avoid application of"])]
              [(EQ (CAR INST) 'NEG)
               (COND
                 [(EQ (GET HNAME 'RECOMMENDATION)
                     'USE)
                  "Do not apply"]
                 [T "Do not avoid application of"])])))
        (GET HNAME 'EVIDENCE))
      (TERPRI)]))

(DE SIMPLIFY* (FRVAL)
  (PROG (OPERANDS NUMERICAL-PRODUCT NON-NUM-OPERANDS)
    (SETQ OPERANDS (MAPCAR 'SIMPLIFY-FR (CDR FRVAL)))
    (SETQ NUMERICAL-PRODUCT 1)
    (RETURN
     (PROGN
       (SETQ OPERANDS
         (DISASSOCIATE-FR '* NIL OPERANDS))
       (MAPC
         (F:L (OPERAND)
           (COND
```

```
          [(NUMBERP OPERAND)
           (SETQ NUMERICAL-PRODUCT
             (* NUMERICAL-PRODUCT OPERAND))]
          [T
           (SETQ NON-NUM-OPERANDS
             (CONS OPERAND NON-NUM-OPERANDS))]))
       OPERANDS)
     (COND
       [(EQ NUMERICAL-PRODUCT 0) 0]
       [(NULL NON-NUM-OPERANDS) NUMERICAL-PRODUCT]
       [(EQ NUMERICAL-PRODUCT 1)
        (COND
          [(EQ (LENGTH NON-NUM-OPERANDS) 1)
           (CAR NON-NUM-OPERANDS)]
          [T (CONS '* NON-NUM-OPERANDS)])]
       [T
        (CONS '*
          (CONS NUMERICAL-PRODUCT NON-NUM-OPERANDS))]))))))

(DE SIMPLIFY+ (FRVAL)
  (PROG (OPERANDS NUMERICAL-SUM NON-NUM-OPERANDS)
    (SETQ OPERANDS (MAPCAR 'SIMPLIFY-FR (CDR FRVAL)))
    (SETQ NUMERICAL-SUM 0)
    (RETURN
     (PROGN
       (SETQ OPERANDS
         (DISASSOCIATE-FR '+ NIL OPERANDS))
       (MAPC
         (F:L (OPERAND)
           (COND
             [(NUMBERP OPERAND)
              (SETQ NUMERICAL-SUM
                (+ NUMERICAL-SUM OPERAND))]
             [T
              (SETQ NON-NUM-OPERANDS
                (CONS OPERAND NON-NUM-OPERANDS))]))
         OPERANDS)
       (COND
         [(NULL NON-NUM-OPERANDS) NUMERICAL-SUM]
         [(EQ NUMERICAL-SUM 0)
          (COND
            [(EQ (LENGTH NON-NUM-OPERANDS) 1)
             (CAR NON-NUM-OPERANDS)]
            [T (CONS '+ NON-NUM-OPERANDS)])]
```

```
          [T
           (CONS '+
             (CONS NUMERICAL-SUM NON-NUM-OPERANDS))])))))

(DE SIMPLIFY- (FRVAL)
  (SIMPLIFY-FR
    (CONS '+
      (CONS
        (CADR FRVAL)
        (MAPCAR
          (F:L (OPERAND) (LIST '* -1 OPERAND))
          (CDDR FRVAL)))))))

(DE SIMPLIFY-FR (FRVAL)
  (COND
    [(ATOM FRVAL) FRVAL]
    [(EQ (CAR FRVAL) '+)       (SIMPLIFY+ FRVAL)]
    [(EQ (CAR FRVAL) '*)       (SIMPLIFY* FRVAL)]
    [(EQ (CAR FRVAL) '-)       (SIMPLIFY- FRVAL)]
    [(EQ (CAR FRVAL) '\)       (SIMPLIFY\ FRVAL)]
    [(EQ (CAR FRVAL) '^)       (SIMPLIFY^ FRVAL)]
    [(EQ (CAR FRVAL) '~)       (SIMPLIFY~ FRVAL)]
    [T
     (MSG "**** unknown fr in simplify-fr: " FRVAL T)
     FRVAL]))

(DE SIMPLIFY\ (FRVAL)
  (SIMPLIFY-FR
    (CONS '*
      (CONS
        (CADR FRVAL)
        (MAPCAR
          (F:L (OPERAND) (LIST '^ OPERAND -1))
          (CDDR FRVAL)))))))

(DE SIMPLIFY^ (FRVAL)
  (PROG (OPERAND1 OPERAND2)
    (SETQ OPERAND1 (SIMPLIFY-FR (CADR FRVAL)))
    (SETQ OPERAND2
      (SIMPLIFY-FR (CONS '* (CDDR FRVAL))))
    (RETURN
     (COND
       [(EQ OPERAND2 0) 1]
       [(EQ OPERAND2 1) OPERAND1]
```

```
       [(AND (NUMBERP OPERAND1) (NUMBERP OPERAND2))
        (^ OPERAND1 OPERAND2)]
       [T (LIST '^ OPERAND1 OPERAND2)])))))

(DE SIMPLIFY~ (FRVAL)
  (PROG (OPERANDS)
    (SETQ OPERANDS (MAPCAR 'SIMPLIFY-FR (CDR FRVAL)))
    (RETURN
     (PROGN
       (SETQ OPERANDS
         (REVERSE
          (DISASSOCIATE-FR '~ NIL OPERANDS)))
       (SETQ OPERANDS
         (SIMPLIFY~OPERANDS-LIST NIL OPERANDS))
       (COND
         [(NULL OPERANDS) 'ID]
         [(EQ (LENGTH OPERANDS) 1) (CAR OPERANDS)]
         [T (CONS '~ OPERANDS)])))))

(DE SIMPLIFY~OPERANDS-LIST (OLDOPS NEWOPS)
  (COND
    [(NULL NEWOPS) (APPEND (REVERSE OLDOPS) NEWOPS)]
    [(NUMBERP (CAR NEWOPS))
     (APPEND (REVERSE OLDOPS) (NCONS (CAR NEWOPS)))]
    [(EQ (CAR NEWOPS) 'ID)
     (SIMPLIFY~OPERANDS-LIST NIL
       (APPEND (REVERSE OLDOPS) (CDR NEWOPS)))]
    [(TEST-INVERSE-FRS (CAR NEWOPS) (CADR NEWOPS))
     (SIMPLIFY~OPERANDS-LIST NIL
       (APPEND (REVERSE OLDOPS) (CDDR NEWOPS)))]
    [T
     (SIMPLIFY~OPERANDS-LIST
       (CONS (CAR NEWOPS) OLDOPS)
       (CDR NEWOPS))]))

(DE SPLICE-MAPS (LMAP RMAP)
  {;; LMAP maps A to B, and RMAP maps B to C.
     Destructively alter LMAP such that it maps A to C.}
  (AND LMAP RMAP
    (WITH [(TEMP
             (COND
               [(EQ (CAR LMAP) '-->)
                (COND
                  [(AND (CONSP (CADDR LMAP))
```

```
                  (MEMQ (CAADDR LMAP) '(--> ==>)))
                 (SPLICE-MAPS (CADDR LMAP) RMAP)]
                [(EQUAL (CADDR LMAP) (CADR RMAP))
                 (RPLACA (CDDR LMAP) RMAP)]
                [T
                 (MSG 0
                   "Unsure how to splice maps "
                   LMAP " and " RMAP T)
                 (HELPME)])]
              [(EQ (CAR LMAP) '==>)
               (COND
                 [(EQUAL (CADDR LMAP) (CADR RMAP))
                  (RPLACA (CDDR LMAP) RMAP)]
                 [T
                  (MSG 0
                    "Unsure how to splice maps "
                    LMAP " and " RMAP T)])]
              [T
               (MSG 0
                 "Ill-formed map in SPLICE-MAPS: "
                 LMAP T)]))]
      LMAP)))

(DE TEST-INVERSE-FRS (FR1 FR2)
  (OR (AND (EQ FR1 'LN) (EQ FR2 'EXP))))

(DE TRIM-ALL-TRAILING-DIGITS (VAL)
  (AND VAL
    (COND
      [(ATOM VAL) (TRIM-TRAILING-DIGITS VAL)]
      [T
       (CONS
         (TRIM-ALL-TRAILING-DIGITS (CAR VAL))
         (TRIM-ALL-TRAILING-DIGITS (CDR VAL)))])))

(DE TRIM-TRAILING-DIGITS (ATOM-NAME)
  (COND
    [(NUMBERP ATOM-NAME) ATOM-NAME]
    [T
     (PROG (CHARS)
       (SETQ CHARS (REVERSE (EXPLODEC ATOM-NAME)))
       (RETURN
        (PROGN
         (DO
```

```
                WHILE
                (NUMBERP (READLIST (NCONS (CAR CHARS))))
                (SETQ CHARS (CDR CHARS)))
             (READLIST (REVERSE CHARS)))))])))

(DE UNMAP-MOST-GENERAL (MAP)
  {;; Removes all MAP info and returns the more specific
      pattern with the more general pattern substituted for
      whatever it mapped to in the more specific pattern.}
  (COND
    [(ATOM MAP) MAP]
    [(MEMQ (CAR MAP) '(--> ==>))
     {;; Aha, the mapped portion}
     (CADR MAP)]
    [T
     (CONS
        (UNMAP-MOST-GENERAL (CAR MAP))
        (UNMAP-MOST-GENERAL (CDR MAP)))]))

(DE UNMAP-MOST-SPECIFIC (MAP)
  {;; Removes all MAP info and returns just the more
      specific pattern.}
  (COND
    [(ATOM MAP) MAP]
    [(EQ (CAR MAP) '-->)
     (UNMAP-MOST-SPECIFIC (CADDR MAP))]
    [(EQ (CAR MAP) '==>)
     (COND
        [(MEMQ (CAADDR MAP) '(--> ==>))
         (UNMAP-MOST-SPECIFIC (CADDR MAP))]
        [T (CADDR MAP)])]
    [T
     (CONS
        (UNMAP-MOST-SPECIFIC (CAR MAP))
        (UNMAP-MOST-SPECIFIC (CDR MAP)))]))

(DE UNTAG-TRIM (PAT)
  (COND
    [(ATOM PAT) (TRIM-TRAILING-DIGITS PAT)]
    [(EQ (CAR PAT) 'TAG)
     (COND
        [(ATOM (CDR PAT)) (TRIM-TRAILING-DIGITS (CDR PAT))]
        [T (CDR PAT)])]
    [T PAT]))
```

```
(DV \PRINTTHRESH 6)

(DE ^ (X Y)
  {;; I defined this because it was not defined in xlisp.
     Furthermore, I couldn't find any function that would do
     exponentiation, so this one does not. - TM 12/80}
  (LIST '^ X Y))
```

Index